# CHARLES SWINDOLL

# Words of Encouragement

*Words of Encouragement*

Copyright © 1996, Daily Blessings
Pentagon Towers, P. O. Box 36024, Edina, MN 55435

Compiled by Benjamin Unseth

SPCN 5-5044-9020-0

There are times I think it might be better to have my future predictable, but looking back, I'm always grateful God didn't tell me ahead of time.

GROWING WISE IN FAMILY LIFE, P. 254

*Now to him who is able to do immeasurably more than all we ask or imagine, according to his power that is at work within us, to him be glory in the church and in Christ Jesus throughout all generations, for ever and ever! Amen.*

EPHESIANS 3:20,21 NIV

JANUARY 1

We've come to the close of another year. But what a feeling to know we're getting stronger and growing tall in God!

GROWING STRONG IN THE SEASONS OF LIFE, P. 73

*But the path of the righteous is like the light of dawn, which shines brighter and brighter until full day.*

PROVERBS 4:18 NRSV

# DECEMBER 31

The church provides perspective that gives dignity to mankind. We live in a day in which man has become a means rather than an end. This creates a desperate sense of inner worthlessness. The church counteracts this insidious message.

COME BEFORE WINTER, P. 257

*Now you are the body of Christ, and each one of you is a part of it.*

1 CORINTHIANS 12:27 NIV

# JANUARY 2

Identify the "danger areas" in your life—those tendencies or weaknesses that carry the greatest hazard of plunging you into sin. Carefully evaluate what activities, situations, or associations during the course of an average week bring you closest to those areas of "thin ice."

GROWING DEEP IN THE CHRISTIAN LIFE, P. 230

*My child, if sinners entice you, do not consent.*
PROVERBS 1:10 NIV

DECEMBER 30

**S**urrendering is not an option if you plan to win a war—or succeed in a marriage.

STRIKE THE ORIGINAL MATCH, P. 31

*What is impossible with men is possible with God.*

LUKE 18:27 NIV

# JANUARY 3

# I challenge you: Release your grip on all those details! Find a few qualified people to help you get the job done.

STRESS FRACTURES, P. 26

*Moses' father-in-law replied, "What you are doing is not good. You and these people who come to you will only wear yourselves out. The work is too heavy for you; you cannot handle it alone."*

EXODUS 18:17,18 NIV

# DECEMBER 29

${\rm B}$y following the model of those who have gone before us, we can do more than survive. We can overcome!

RISE AND SHINE, P. 175

*With us is the Lord our God to help us, and to fight our battles.*

2 CHRONICLES 32:8 KJV

JANUARY 4

Apart from the Way there is no going—apart from the Truth there is no knowing—apart from the Life there is no living.

GROWING STRONG IN THE SEASONS OF LIFE, P. 322

*Jesus answered, "I am the way and the truth and the life. No one comes to the Father except through me."*

JOHN 14:6 NIV

DECEMBER 28

The permanent peace and pleasure you are enjoying with Christ is so much greater than [sin's] temporary excitement that you don't need it around any longer to keep you happy.

COME BEFORE WINTER, P. 32

*You have made known to me the path of life; you will fill me with joy in your presence, with eternal pleasures at your right hand.*

PSALM 16:11 NIV

# JANUARY 5

When the wrappings and ribbons are in the trash, the manger scene is back in the attic, the friends and family have said good-bye, and the house feels empty and so do you—there is One who waits to fill your heart and renew your hope.

COME BEFORE WINTER, P. 214

*Praise be to the God and Father of our Lord Jesus Christ! In his great mercy he has given us new birth into a living hope through the resurrection of Jesus Christ from the dead.*

1 PETER 1:3 NIV

# DECEMBER 27

You are absolutely secure in the everlasting arms of your eternal Savior. In Him, you are safe!

STRESS FRACTURES, P. 252

*The eternal God is thy refuge, and underneath are the everlasting arms.*

DEUTERONOMY 33:27 KJV

JANUARY 6

Reeling from the wake of Alexander the Great—
Herod the Great—Augustus the Great, the world
overlooked Mary's little Lamb. It still does.

GROWING STRONG IN THE SEASONS OF LIFE, P. 51

*He was in the world, and though the world was made through him,
the world did not recognize him. He came to that which
was his own, but his own did not receive him.*

JOHN 1:10,11 NIV

# DECEMBER 26

The church is a family, not a business. Businesses don't have fathers and mothers; families do. The flock of God is not a corporation gone public.

RISE AND SHINE, P. 89

*As we preached God's Good News among you...we talked to you as a father to his own children.*

1 THESSALONIANS 2:9,11 TLB

JANUARY 7

While Rome was busy making history, God arrived. He pitched His fleshly tent in silence on straw—in a stable—under a star. The world didn't even notice.

GROWING STRONG IN THE SEASONS OF LIFE, P. 51

*The Word became flesh and made his dwelling among us.*
*We have seen his glory, the glory of the One and Only,*
*who came from the Father, full of grace and truth.*

JOHN 1:14 NIV

DECEMBER 25

What do you need when circumstances puncture your fragile dikes and threaten to engulf your life with pain and confusion? You need a shelter. A listener. Someone who understands.

GROWING STRONG IN THE SEASONS OF LIFE, P. 377

*In you, O Lord, I have taken refuge.... Turn your ear to me, come quickly to my rescue; be my rock of refuge, a strong fortress to save me.*

PSALM 31:1,2 NIV

JANUARY 8

It's important that we rivet into our heads exactly what we're celebrating. It is our Savior's arrival, not Santa's.

COME BEFORE WINTER, P. 213

*When the time had fully come, God sent his Son, born of a woman, born under law, to redeem those under the law, that we might receive the full rights of sons.*

GALATIANS 4:4 NIV

# DECEMBER 24

## CONSISTENCY

It's the jewel worth wearing.
It's the anchor worth weighing.
It's the thread worth weaving.
It's the battle worth winning.

GROWING STRONG IN THE SEASONS OF LIFE, P. 27

*Let us not be weary in well doing: for in due season
we shall reap, if we faint not.*

GALATIANS 6:9 KJV

# JANUARY 9

Joseph cleaned up from the birth and put that little tiny life into a rough feeding trough. Mary looked down and saw God by her side.

GROWING DEEP IN THE CHRISTIAN LIFE, P. 129

*The virgin will be with child and will give birth to a son, and they will call him Immanuel—which means, "God with us."*

MATTHEW 1:23 NIV

# DECEMBER 23

Consciously start taking time for leisure.
After God put the world together, He rested.
We are commanded to imitate Him.

STRESS FRACTURES, P. 170

*In six days the Lord made heaven and earth, and on*
*the seventh day he rested, and was refreshed.*

EXODUS 31:17 KJV

JANUARY 10

In charge of the Roman world, Augustus had no earthly idea that a teenaged pregnant girl named Mary living in Nazareth was about to bear a son named Jesus. But the world was about to find out that infant named Jesus was really the significance of that era, not Caesar.

GROWING DEEP IN THE CHRISTIAN LIFE, P. 124

*Caesar Augustus issued a decree that a census should be taken of the entire Roman world. So Joseph also went up from the town of Nazareth...to register with Mary, who was pledged to be married to him and was expecting a child.*

LUKE 2:1,4,5 NIV

DECEMBER 22

Do you know of someone who could and should be promoted to a place of greater usefulness, but is presently in need of your companionship and confidence? Go to bat for him! Stand in his stead. Give him a boost. He needs your fellowship.

GROWING STRONG IN THE SEASONS OF LIFE, P. 215

*Let us run with perseverance the race marked out for us.*
*Let us fix our eyes on Jesus, the author and perfecter of our faith.*

HEBREWS 12:1,2 NIV

# JANUARY 11

There was a tiny Lamb in Bethlehem who was destined for Golgotha's altar.

GROWING DEEP IN THE CHRISTIAN LIFE, P. 130

*You were ransomed...with the precious blood of Christ, like that of a lamb without defect or blemish. He was destined before the foundation of the world.*

I PETER 1:18-20 NRSV

# DECEMBER 21

# Holiness sounds scary. It needn't be, but to the average American, it is.

STRESS FRACTURES, P. 94

*We have been made holy through the sacrifice of the body of Jesus Christ once for all.*

HEBREWS 10:10 NIV

JANUARY 12

Without adding sufficient leisure time to our schedule for meaningful communication, a relationship with those who are important to us will disintegrate faster than we can keep it in repair.

STRESS FRACTURES, P. 165

*Six days do your work, but on the seventh day do not work, so that [all] may be refreshed.*

EXODUS 23:12 NIV

DECEMBER 20

God continues to hold out to all His children a peaceful, worry-free lifestyle that we can enter into on a moment by moment basis.

STRESS FRACTURES, P. 29

*There remains, then, a Sabbath-rest for the people of God.*

HEBREWS 4:9 NIV

JANUARY 13

**R**UN! It is impossible to yield to temptation while running in the opposite direction.

STRESS FRACTURES, P. 124

*And [Potiphar's wife] caught [Joseph] by his cloak and said, "Come to bed with me!" But he left his cloak in her hand and ran out of the house.*

GENESIS 39:12 NIV

DECEMBER 19

God never promised you a Disneyland. He offers something better—His own sustaining presence through any trouble you may encounter.

COME BEFORE WINTER, PP. 181-182

*I will never leave thee, nor forsake thee.*

HEBREWS 13:5 KJV

JANUARY 14

The avoidance of legitimate suffering means we also avoid the growth that problems demand of us.

GROWING STRONG IN THE SEASONS OF LIFE, P. 125

*But he knows the way that I take; when he has tested me,
I will come forth as gold.*

JOB 23:10 NIV

# DECEMBER 18

When will we learn that efficiency is enhanced not by what we accomplish but more often by what we relinquish?

GROWING STRONG IN THE SEASONS OF LIFE, P. 262

*When Jesus heard this, he said to him, "You still lack one thing. Sell everything you have and give to the poor, and you will have treasure in heaven. Then come, follow me."*

LUKE 18:22 NIV

# JANUARY 15

T he better we know His Word, the more
clearly we will know His will.

STRESS FRACTURES, P. 241

*I have hidden your word in my heart that
I might not sin against you.*

PSALM 119:11 NIV

# DECEMBER 17

Do you know Christ Jesus—I mean really know Him?
If so, RUN. Fix your eyes on Him and refuse to give up
or turn back. If not, STOP. Give Him your struggles
and receive Him by faith.

STARTING OVER, P. 77

*Let us run with perseverance the race marked out for us. Let us
fix our eyes on Jesus, the author and perfecter of our faith.*

HEBREWS 12:1,2 NIV

# JANUARY 16

Learn your lessons well in the schoolroom of obscurity. God is preparing you as His chosen arrow. As yet your shaft is hidden in His quiver, but at the precise moment at which it will tell with the greatest effect, He will reach for you and launch you to that place of His appointment.

GROWING STRONG IN THE SEASONS OF LIFE, P. 531

*In the shadow of his hand he hid me; he made me into a polished arrow and concealed me in his quiver.*

ISAIAH 49:2 NIV

# DECEMBER 16

More often than not it is in the quiet, unnoticed, unapplauded realms of life that one demonstrates integrity—within the walls of one's own home—in the secret chambers of one's own heart.

RISE AND SHINE, P. 194

*Create in me a pure heart, O God, and renew a steadfast spirit within me.*

PSALM 51:10 NIV

# JANUARY 17

Generosity is like a rare gem. Not many of us possess it, but when it is seen it sparkles. What admiration it brings from onlookers. Are you sparkling today? Or have you misplaced the gem called generosity?

GROWING STRONG IN THE SEASONS OF LIFE, P. 406

*A generous man will prosper; he who refreshes others will himself be refreshed.*

PROVERBS 11:25 NIV

# DECEMBER 15

There can be no more reliable authority on earth than God's Word, the Bible. This timeless, trustworthy source of truth holds the key that unlocks life's mysteries. It alone provides us with the shelter we need in times of storm.

GROWING DEEP IN THE CHRISTIAN LIFE, P. 55

*For everything that was written in the past was written to teach us, so that through endurance and the encouragement of the Scriptures we might have hope.*

ROMANS 15:4 NIV

JANUARY 18

A balanced woman of God sees herself as valuable, gifted, responsible for her own growth and maturity— not overly dependent on anyone to get her through life or to make her secure.

STRESS FRACTURES, P. 147

*She considers a field and buys it; out of her earnings she plants a vineyard.... She sees that her trading is profitable, and her lamp does not go out at night.*

PROVERBS 31:16,18 NIV

# DECEMBER 14

Logical thinking will discourage you;
theological thinking will encourage you.

STRESS FRACTURES, P. 222

*It is unthinkable that God would do wrong, that
the Almighty would pervert justice.*

JOB 34:12 NIV

JANUARY 19

A balanced woman of God sees Scripture as God's vital and relevant Word, worth her attention, devotion, and application.

STRESS FRACTURES, P. 146

*Train the younger women to love their husbands and children, to be self-controlled and pure.*

TITUS 2:4,5 NIV

DECEMBER 13

The real you—that which God develops—
is within you.

GROWING STRONG IN THE SEASONS OF LIFE, P. 141

*A good man out of the good treasure of his heart bringeth forth
that which is good...for of the abundance of the heart
his mouth speaketh.*

LUKE 6:45 KJV

JANUARY 20

Peter's advice could be summarized in three short statements: dwell with your wife; know the woman you live with; give her honor.

STRESS FRACTURES, P. 146

*Husbands...be considerate as you live with your wives, and treat them with respect...and as heirs with you of the gracious gift of life, so that nothing will hinder your prayers.*

1 PETER 3:7 NIV

DECEMBER 12

It's okay to relax. It's essential!

STRESS FRACTURES, P. 155

*For my yoke is easy, and my burden is light.*

MATTHEW 11:30 KJV

JANUARY 21

Hooray for Timothy's roots! The sincere faith that ultimately marked Timothy's life first resided in his grandmother, Lois, and his mother, Eunice.

RISE AND SHINE, P. 161

*I know how much you trust the Lord just as your mother Eunice and your grandmother Lois do; and I feel sure you are still trusting him as much as ever.*

2 TIMOTHY 1:5 TLB

# DECEMBER 11

God has somehow placed into the Christian's insides a special something, that extra inner reservoir of power that is more than a match for the stuff life throws at us. When in operation, phenomenal accomplishments are achieved, sometimes even miraculous.

COME BEFORE WINTER, P. 134

*I can do all things through Christ who strengthens me.*

PHILIPPIANS 4:13 NKJV

JANUARY 22

Love and commitment deepen as two people work toward common goals in a marriage.

STRESS FRACTURES, P. 145

*Do two walk together unless they have agreed to do so?*

AMOS 3:3 NIV

DECEMBER 10

$I$ firmly believe that an individual is never more Christ-like than when full of compassion for those who are down, needy, discouraged, or forgotten. How terribly essential is our commitment to encouragement!

GROWING STRONG IN THE SEASONS OF LIFE, P. 213

*Encourage one another daily, as long as it is called Today.*

HEBREWS 3:13 NIV

JANUARY 23

Good never intended the woman to feel inferior or to live fearfully beneath some heavy cloud of unfair domination.

STRESS FRACTURES, P. 143

*Women...have contended at my side in the cause of the gospel.*

PHILIPPIANS 4:3 NIV

DECEMBER 9

Give the dreamers room. Go easy on the "shouldn'ts" and the "can'ts," okay? Dreams are fragile things that have a hard time emerging in a cloud of negativism—reminders like "no money," and "too many problems."

THE QUEST FOR CHARACTER, P. 171

*For with God nothing shall be impossible.*

LUKE 1:37 KJV

# JANUARY 24

The women who appear in Scripture are competent, secure, qualified people who had responsible roles to fill.

STRESS FRACTURES, P. 141

*A woman who fears the Lord is to be praised. Give her the reward she has earned, and let her works bring her praise at the city gate.*

PROVERBS 31:30,31 NIV

DECEMBER 8

$S$alvation is simply a gift. It's simple, but it wasn't easy. It's free, but it wasn't cheap. It's yours, but it isn't automatic. You must receive it. When you do, it is yours forever.

GROWING DEEP IN THE CHRISTIAN LIFE, P. 244

*For you know that it was not with perishable things such as silver or gold that you were redeemed from the empty way of life handed down to you from your forefathers, but with the precious blood of Christ, a lamb without blemish or defect.*

I PETER 1:18,19 NIV

JANUARY 25

I know of nothing more effective for maintaining a pure heart and keeping one's life balanced and on target than being a part of an accountability group.

RISE AND SHINE, P. 211

*As iron sharpens iron, so one man sharpens another.*

PROVERBS 27:17 NIV

DECEMBER 7

It is the simple truth that holds you together in the most complex situations. Not simplistic, but simple. The profound truth that the Bible gives us is like a warm blanket wrapped around us on a cold night.

GROWING DEEP IN THE CHRISTIAN LIFE, P. 66

*A faith and knowledge resting on the hope of eternal life, which God, who does not lie, promised before the beginning of time.*

TITUS 1:2 NIV

# JANUARY 26

Today our living Lord welcomes you into His presence. Even though you may admit to some reluctance, God nevertheless awaits those few precious moments when you lift your face and heart to Him.

THE QUEST FOR CHARACTER, P. 124

*Therefore...we have confidence to enter the Most Holy Place by the blood of Jesus.*

HEBREWS 10:19 NIV

# DECEMBER 6

Happiness, like winning, is a matter of right thinking,
not intelligence, age, or position.

COME BEFORE WINTER, P. 239

*Finally, brothers, whatever is true, whatever is noble, whatever is right,
whatever is pure, whatever is lovely, whatever is admirable—if anything
is excellent or praiseworthy—think about such things.*

PHILIPPIANS 4:8 NIV

JANUARY 27

Having some big struggles with envy? Eating your heart out because somebody's a step or two ahead of you in the race and gaining momentum? Relax. You are you—not them!

COME BEFORE WINTER, P. 99

*Listen, my son, and be wise, and keep your heart on the right path.*

PROVERBS 23:19 NIV

# DECEMBER 5

Lord, right now, at this moment, I am weak. You're strong. By Your strength I'm stepping away from this evil, and Your power is going to give me the grace to get through it victoriously. Take charge right now.

GROWING DEEP IN THE CHRISTIAN LIFE, P. 228

*And he said unto me, My grace is sufficient for thee: for my strength is made perfect in weakness. Most gladly therefore will I rather glory in my infirmities, that the power of Christ may rest upon me.*

2 CORINTHIANS 12:9 KJV

# JANUARY 28

If I could have only one wish for God's people, it would be that all of us would return to the Word of God, that we would realize that His Book has the answers. The Bible is the authority, the final resting place of our cares, worries, griefs, tragedies, sorrows, and our surprises. It is the final answer to our questions, our search.

GROWING DEEP IN THE CHRISTIAN LIFE, P. 56

*If your law had not been my delight, I would have perished in my affliction.*

PSALM 119:92 NIV

# DECEMBER 4

Whoever you may be tempted to reject, don't reject Christ, the Lord! He is the only One who is absolutely perfect—the only One who can guarantee you a home in heaven. He is the only One who can forgive your sins.

RISE AND SHINE, P. 237

*God made him who had no sin to be sin for us, so that in him we might become the righteousness of God.*

2 CORINTHIANS 5:21 NIV

JANUARY 29

We will have no more tears, no more death, no more sadness, no more crying, no more disease, no more temptations, no more deformity or struggle with Satan. No more paralysis or crippling diseases. None of that! All those things are passed away as eternity dawns.

GROWING DEEP IN THE CHRISTIAN LIFE, P. 303

*He will wipe every tear from their eyes. There will be no more death or mourning or crying or pain, for the old order of things has passed away.*

REVELATION 21:4 NIV

# DECEMBER 3

His Word provides the truth I need. It erases the doubts, it gives a sure footing even though I am surrounded by people in a swamp of uncertainty.

GROWING DEEP IN THE CHRISTIAN LIFE, P. 60

*He remembers his covenant forever, the word he commanded, for a thousand generations.*

I CHRONICLES 16:15 NIV

JANUARY 30

We are God's personal projects. The emerging
of the Son's image in us is of primary
importance to the Father.

COME BEFORE WINTER, P. 335

*We all, with open face beholding as in a glass the glory of the Lord,
are changed into the same image from glory to glory, even as
by the Spirit of the Lord.*

2 CORINTHIANS 3:18 KJV

DECEMBER 2

There is no more significant involvement in another's life than prevailing, consistent prayer. It is more helpful than a gift of money, more encouraging than a strong sermon, more effective than a compliment, more reassuring than a physical embrace.

THE QUEST FOR CHARACTER, P. 132

*As for me, God forbid that I should sin against the Lord in ceasing to pray for you.*

1 SAMUEL 12:23 KJV

JANUARY 31

Can't find a refuge? Why not share David's shelter?
The One he called My Strength, Mighty Rock,
Fortress, Stronghold, and High Tower.

GROWING STRONG IN THE SEASONS OF LIFE, P. 380

*The God of my rock; in him will I trust: he is my shield, and the horn of my salvation, my high tower, and my refuge, my saviour.*

2 SAMUEL 22:3 KJV

# DECEMBER 1

Jesus promised people "rest" if they would come to Him, not an endless list of unrealistic expectations.

GROWING STRONG IN THE SEASONS OF LIFE, P. 333

*Come to me, all you who are weary and burdened, and I will give you rest.*

MATTHEW 11:28 NIV

# FEBRUARY 1

Crying is the most natural response when we lose someone or something important to us. We have every reason to grieve and to be sad, but our grief is not as the hopeless when they grieve. You see, we have an answer beyond the grave.

GROWING DEEP IN THE CHRISTIAN LIFE, P. 275

*But God will redeem my life from the grave;*
*he will surely take me to himself.*

PSALM 49:15 NIV

NOVEMBER 30

God doesn't mock us. He never gives a goal that we cannot accomplish in His strength. I want to assure you, you can glorify God—you must glorify God.

RISE AND SHINE, P. 35

*Because your love is better than life, my lips will glorify you.*

PSALM 63:3 NIV

# FEBRUARY 2

As we marvel at God's handiwork among His creatures, we gain a renewed respect for His creative genius.

GROWING STRONG IN THE SEASONS OF LIFE, P. 174

*The heavens declare the glory of God;*
*the skies proclaim the work of his hands.*

PSALM 19:1 NIV

# NOVEMBER 29

Discernment will act as a watchdog to keep us from getting lost in the morass of tomorrow's depravity and deception even as we keep pace with its advancements.

RISE AND SHINE, P. 142

*A rich man may be wise in his own eyes, but a poor man who has discernment sees through him.*

PROVERBS 28:11 NIV

FEBRUARY 3

Thank you, Lord, that I have a few things worth giving.
Even if it's a lap to be sat on...or the comfort
of a warm embrace.

GROWING STRONG IN THE SEASONS OF LIFE, P. 592

*Each of you should look not only to your own interests,*
*but also to the interests of others.*

PHILIPPIANS 2:4 NIV

NOVEMBER 28

Criticism challenges it—adventure arouses it—danger incites it—threats quicken it. Courage—another word for inner strength, presence of mind against odds, determination to hang in there, to venture, persevere, withstand hardship.

GROWING STRONG IN THE SEASONS OF LIFE, PP. 542-543

*I eagerly expect and hope that I will in no way be ashamed, but will have sufficient courage so that now as always Christ will be exalted in my body, whether by life or by death.*

PHILIPPIANS 1:20 NIV

FEBRUARY 4

The meal, the memories, the music Thanksgiving brings have a way of blocking out the gaunt giant of selfishness and ushering in the sincere spirit of gratitude, love, and genuine joy.

GROWING STRONG IN THE SEASONS OF LIFE, P. 580

*Oh that men would praise the Lord for his goodness, and for his wonderful works to the children of men!*

PSALM 107:15 KJV

NOVEMBER 27

The ideal gift is...yourself. Give an hour of your time. Give a note of encouragement. Give a hug of affirmation. Give a visit of mercy. Give a meal you prepared. Give a word of compassion. Give a deed of kindness.

THE QUEST FOR CHARACTER, P. 177

*I do not want to see you now and make only a passing visit; I hope to spend some time with you, if the Lord permits.*

I CORINTHIANS 16:7 NIV

# FEBRUARY 5

Thanksgiving is a time of quiet reflection upon the past and an annual reminder that God has, again, been ever so faithful. The solid and simple things of life are brought into clear focus, so much so that everything else fades into insignificance.

GROWING STRONG IN THE SEASONS OF LIFE, P. 579

*Look to the Lord and his strength; seek his face always. Remember the wonders he has done.*

PSALM 105:4,5 NIV

# NOVEMBER 26

Accept it or not, God's calling the shots. He's running the show. Either He's in full control or He's off His throne.

GROWING STRONG IN THE SEASONS OF LIFE, P. 396

*All the peoples of the earth are regarded as nothing. He does as he pleases with the powers of heaven and the peoples of the earth. No one can hold back his hand.*

DANIEL 4:35 NIV

FEBRUARY 6

At this holiday, as at no other, we count our blessings and we run out of time before we exhaust the list.

GROWING STRONG IN THE SEASONS OF LIFE, P. 582

*Give thanks in all circumstances, for this is God's will for you in Christ Jesus.*

1 THESSALONIANS 5:18 NIV

# NOVEMBER 25

God is too kind to do anything cruel. Too wise to make a mistake. Too deep to explain himself.

GROWING STRONG IN THE SEASONS OF LIFE, P. 135

*Can you fathom the mysteries of God? Can you probe the limits of the Almighty? They are higher than the heavens.... They are deeper than the depths of the grave.... Their measure is longer than the earth and wider than the sea.*

JOB 11:7-9 NIV

FEBRUARY 7

Thanksgiving speaks in clear, crisp tones of forgotten terms, like integrity—bravery—respect—faith—vigilance—dignity—honor—freedom—discipline—sacrifice—godliness.

GROWING STRONG IN THE SEASONS OF LIFE, P. 581

*May you be made strong with all the strength that comes from his glorious power...while joyfully giving thanks to the Father.*

COLOSSIANS 1:11,12 NRSV

# NOVEMBER 23

The worst place in the world to be
when going through doubts is all alone.
You need a friend to support you.

STRESS FRACTURES, P. 66

*If one falls down, his friend can help him up. But pity
the man who falls and has no one to help him up!*

ECCLESIASTES 4:10 NIV

FEBRUARY 9

Hands down, Thanksgiving is my favorite holiday. It highlights the home and family. It is synonymous with stuff that can be found only at home—early morning fussing around in the kitchen, kids and grandkids, long distance phone calls, holding hands and praying before that special meal.

GROWING STRONG IN THE SEASONS OF LIFE, P. 579

*From everlasting to everlasting the Lord's love is with those who fear him, and his righteousness with their children's children.*

PSALM 103:17 NIV

# NOVEMBER 22

Look for things to laugh at—and
laugh out loud. It's biblical!

STRESS FRACTURES, P. 168

*A merry heart does good, like medicine,*
*but a broken spirit dries the bones.*

PROVERBS 17:22 NKJV

FEBRUARY 10

If God thought that this planet needed several months of summer, it stands to reason that His people are equally in need of refreshment and rest.

GROWING STRONG IN THE SEASONS OF LIFE, P. 312

*I will refresh the weary and satisfy the faint.*

JEREMIAH 31:25 NIV

NOVEMBER 21

Let a few people enter into that lonely experience with you. They can stand by you and provide an enormous amount of support, relieving much of the stress you would otherwise be enduring alone.

STRESS FRACTURES, P. 27

*But select capable men from all the people—men who fear God....*
*That will make your load lighter, because they will share it with you.*

EXODUS 18:21,22 NIV

FEBRUARY 11

One of the marks of spiritual maturity is the quiet confidence that God is in control—without the need to understand why He does what He does.

STARTING OVER, P. 69

*Our God is in heaven; he does whatever pleases him.*

PSALM 115:3 NIV

# NOVEMBER 20

# Had it not been for "nobodies"—a huge chunk of church history would be missing. Don't mistake anonymous for unnecessary.

GROWING STRONG IN THE SEASONS OF LIFE, P. 128

*On the contrary, those parts of the body that seem to be weaker are indispensable.*

1 CORINTHIANS 12:22 NIV

# FEBRUARY 12

I am deeply indebted to the man who raised me. Certain smells and sounds now instantly remind me of my dad. Oyster stew. The ocean breeze. Smoke from an expensive cigar. The nostalgic whine of a harmonica. A camping lantern and white gas.

COME BEFORE WINTER, P. 231

*The righteous man leads a blameless life; blessed are his children after him.*

PROVERBS 20:7 NIV

# NOVEMBER 19

Thank the Lord, it is His love that arranges our tomorrows—and we may be certain that whatever tomorrow brings, His love sent it our way.

GROWING STRONG IN THE SEASONS OF LIFE, P. 237

*O the depth of the riches both of the wisdom and knowledge of God! how unsearchable are his judgments, and his ways past finding out!*

ROMANS 11:33 KJV

FEBRUARY 13

Don't let the speed of today cause you to treat the depth of your past lightly. Return to the truth of your past. Review those lives and those events. Remember them, renew them, rely on them, then relay the truth on to your children.

RISE AND SHINE, P. 162

*These commandments that I give you today are to be upon your hearts. Impress them on your children. Talk about them when you sit at home and when you walk along the road, when you lie down and when you get up.*

DEUTERONOMY 6:6,7 NIV

# NOVEMBER 18

There is not an achievement worth remembering that isn't stained with the blood of diligence and etched with the scars of disappointment.

COME BEFORE WINTER, P. 181

*I want to know Christ and the power of his resurrection and the fellowship of sharing in his sufferings, becoming like him in his death.*

PHILIPPIANS 3:10 NIV

# FEBRUARY 14

Character traits are sculptured under the watchful eyes of moms and dads. Purity. "Reject anything that lowers your standards." Compassion. "When another hurts, feel it with him." Diligence. "Work hard. Tough it out."

GROWING STRONG IN THE SEASONS OF LIFE, P. 392

*Listen to your father, who gave you life, and do not despise your mother when she is old.*

PROVERBS 23:22 NIV

NOVEMBER 17

$S$elf-pity is the smog that pollutes and obscures the light of the Son. The more you're out in it, the deeper it hurts. The more your eyes shed tears, the greater the sting of loneliness.

GROWING STRONG IN THE SEASONS OF LIFE, P. 337

*Each of you should look not only to your own interests,*
*but also to the interests of others.*

PHILIPPIANS 2:4 NIV

FEBRUARY 15

Character traits are sculptured under the watchful eyes of moms and dads. Confidentiality. "Don't tell secrets." Punctuality. "Be on time." Self-control. "When under stress, stay calm." Patience. "Fight irritability. Be willing to wait."

GROWING STRONG IN THE SEASONS OF LIFE, P. 392

*Honor your father and your mother: that your days may be long upon the land which the Lord your God is giving you.*

EXODUS 20:12 NKJV

NOVEMBER 16

Is there any hope for lost sinners? Yes, Christ. Not Christ and the church. Not Christ and good works. Not Christ and sincerity. Not Christ and giving up your sins. Not Christ and trying real hard. Not Christ and baptism, Christ and christening, Christ and morality, or Christ and a good family. No! Christ PERIOD!

GROWING DEEP IN THE CHRISTIAN LIFE, P. 243

*I am the way and the truth and the life. No one comes to the Father except through me.*

JOHN 14:6 NIV

# FEBRUARY 16

Character traits are sculptured under the watchful eyes of moms and dads. Determination. "Stick with it, regardless." Honesty. "Speak and live the truth—always." Responsibility. "Be dependable, be trustworthy." Thoughtfulness. "Think of others before yourself."

GROWING STRONG IN THE SEASONS OF LIFE, P. 392

*A man who loves wisdom brings joy to his father.*

PROVERBS 29:3 NIV

# NOVEMBER 15

Peace is the ability to remain faithful in spite
of the panic of unfulfilled dreams.

STRESS FRACTURES, P. 41

*The Lord will fulfill His purpose for me; your love, O Lord,*
*endures forever—do not abandon the works of your hands.*

PSALM 138:8 NIV

FEBRUARY 17

We tend to forget when we're tempted: God is there through it all. He is faithful. We may feel alone, but we are not alone. He places definite limitations on the attack.

STRESS FRACTURES, P. 129

*There hath no temptation taken you but such as is common to man: but God is faithful, who will not suffer you to be tempted above that ye are able; but will with the temptation also make a way to escape, that ye may be able to bear it.*

1 CORINTHIANS 10:13 KJV

NOVEMBER 14

Never underestimate the value of [a handshake].
The handshake is one of a rare remaining species
threatened with extinction in the family of touch.

ENCOURAGE ME, P. 70

*They shook hands with Barnabas and me and encouraged us.*

GALATIANS 2:9 TLB

FEBRUARY 18

Davidʼs Refuge never failed. Not even once. And David
never regretted the times he dropped his heavy load
and ran for cover. Neither will you.

GROWING STRONG IN THE SEASONS OF LIFE, P. 380

*Those who know your name will trust in you, for you, Lord,*
*have never forsaken those who seek you.*

PSALM 9:10 NIV

# NOVEMBER 13

In heaven we'll have a face-to-face, exclusive relationship with our Savior.

STRESS FRACTURES, P. 187

*Now we see but a poor reflection as in a mirror; then we shall see face to face. Now I know in part; then I shall know fully, even as I am fully known.*

1 CORINTHIANS 13:12 NIV

FEBRUARY 19

Dear Father in Heaven, Thank You for the benefits
of pain and suffering. Enable us to learn and
never forget what You are teaching us. Amen.

STRESS FRACTURES, P. 68

*I have refined you, though not as silver;
I have tested you in the furnace of affliction.*

ISAIAH 48:10 NIV

NOVEMBER 12

**W**hen it comes to your emotions, be tough rather than tender. Refuse to let your feelings dominate your mind when lust craves satisfaction.

STRESS FRACTURES, P. 127

*Above all else, guard your affections.*
*For they influence everything else in your life.*

PROVERBS 4:23 TLB

FEBRUARY 20

God is in control of the times and seasons.
Some times are hard, and some seasons are dry.
So the conclusion is: God is in control of
hard times and dry seasons.

STRESS FRACTURES, P. 221

*Though the fig tree does not blossom, and no fruit is on the vines; though
the produce of the olive fails and the fields yield no food; though the flock
is cut off from the fold and there is no herd in the stalls, yet I will rejoice
in the Lord; I will exult in the God of my salvation.*

HABAKKUK 3:17,18 NRSV

# NOVEMBER 11

Closed doors are just as much God's leading
as open ones.

STRESS FRACTURES, P. 243

*When [Paul and his companions] came to the border of Mysia, they
tried to enter Bithynia, but the Spirit of Jesus would not allow them to.
During the night Paul had a vision of a man of Macedonia standing
and begging him, "Come over to Macedonia and help us."*

ACTS 16:7,9 NIV

FEBRUARY 21

# God originally designed and "prescribed" you.

GROWING STRONG IN THE SEASONS OF LIFE, P. 141

*Before I formed you in the womb I knew you,*
*before you were born I set you apart.*

JEREMIAH 1:5 NIV

# NOVEMBER 10

# When love flows, acceptance grows.

GROWING STRONG IN THE SEASONS OF LIFE, P. 415

*Accept one another, then, just as Christ accepted you,*
*in order to bring praise to God.*

ROMANS 15:7 NIV

# FEBRUARY 22

**W**hatever leisure time we are able to invest
in relationships is time well spent.

STRESS FRACTURES, P. 169

*Let us not give up meeting together, as some are in the habit of doing,*
*but let us encourage one another.*

HEBREWS 10:25 NIV

# NOVEMBER 9

$A$n anniversary says, "Think of the dreams you have weathered together. They are intimate accomplishments."

GROWING STRONG IN THE SEASONS OF LIFE, P. 329

*I am my beloved's and my beloved is mine.*

SONG OF SOLOMON 6:3 NRSV

# FEBRUARY 23

Before you consider your case as hopeless, take an honest look at men and women whom God used in spite of their past! Abraham was once a worshiper of idols. Joseph had a prison record. Moses was a murderer. Rahab was a harlot. Eli and Samuel were both poor, inconsistent fathers. Jonah ran away.

GROWING STRONG IN THE SEASONS OF LIFE, P. 373

*These were all commended for their faith.*

HEBREWS 11:39 NIV

# NOVEMBER 8

When we are lonely, we need to lift our eyes off ourselves. Jesus, the "Founder and Finisher" of the life of faith, invites us to fix our eyes on Him and refuse to succumb.

GROWING STRONG IN THE SEASONS OF LIFE, P. 211

*Consider him who endured such opposition from sinful men, so that you will not grow weary and lose heart.*

HEBREWS 12:3 NIV

FEBRUARY 24

God is a Specialist when the anguish is deep. His ability to heal the soul is profound—but only those who rely on His wounded Son will experience relief.

GROWING STRONG IN THE SEASONS OF LIFE, P. 211

*He was wounded for our transgressions, he was bruised for our iniquities; the chastisement of our peace was upon him, and with his stripes we are healed.*

ISAIAH 53:5 KJV

NOVEMBER 7

A ny home can be restored, rebuilt.
It is never too late.

STRIKE THE ORIGINAL MATCH, P. 22

*With men it is impossible, but not with God:
for with God all things are possible.*

MARK 10:27 KJV

# FEBRUARY 25

Christianity is completely credible. Objective, honest, historically documented evidence in favor of the basics of our faith is massive in fact and impressive in volume.

COME BEFORE WINTER, P. 124

*Many have undertaken to draw up an account of the things that have been fulfilled among us, just as they were handed down to us by those who from the first were eyewitnesses and servants of the word.*

LUKE 1:1,2 NIV

# NOVEMBER 6

You are responsible to do the best you can with what you've got for as long as you're able.

COME BEFORE WINTER, P. 99

*As long as it is day, we must do the work of him who sent me.*
*Night is coming, when no one can work.*

JOHN 9:4 NIV

FEBRUARY 26

Some folks feverishly work right up to the deadline on every assignment or project they undertake. Time management allows room for ease and humor, much needed oil to soothe the friction created by motion.

COME BEFORE WINTER, P. 24

*The plans of the diligent lead to profit as surely as haste leads to poverty.*

PROVERBS 21:5 NIV

# NOVEMBER 5

Hope in the future takes the sting out of the present. Life won't be so hard if we learn to live in the conscious hope of Christ's soon return.

GROWING DEEP IN THE CHRISTIAN LIFE, P. 293

*But our citizenship is in heaven. And we eagerly await a Savior from there, the Lord Jesus Christ, who, by the power that enables him to bring everything under his control, will transform our lowly bodies so that they will be like his glorious body.*

PHILIPPIANS 3:20,21 NIV

FEBRUARY 27

Our performance is directly related to the thoughts we deposit in our memory banks. We can only draw on what we deposit.

COME BEFORE WINTER, P. 239

*Receive my instruction, and not silver; and knowledge rather than choice gold.*

PROVERBS 8:10 KJV

# NOVEMBER 4

**W**hen the believer dies, the body goes into the grave; the soul and spirit go immediately to be with the Lord Jesus awaiting the body's resurrection, when they're joined together to be forever with the Lord in eternal bliss.

GROWING DEEP IN THE CHRISTIAN LIFE, P. 308

*Jesus answered him, "I tell you the truth, today you will be with me in paradise."*

LUKE 23:43 NIV

# FEBRUARY 28

The wonderful thing about relying on God's Book is that it gives you stability. It gives you that deep sense of purpose and meaning, even when you get the phone call in the middle of the night. No other counsel will get you through in the long haul like the stability that comes from God's Book.

GROWING DEEP IN THE CHRISTIAN LIFE, P. 65

*The grass withereth, the flower fadeth: but the word of our God shall stand for ever.*

ISAIAH 40:8 KJV

# NOVEMBER 3

What will make your Christianity authentic? It isn't a Sunday lifestyle! It is a Monday, Tuesday, Wednesday, Thursday, Friday, Saturday, Sunday, Monday, Tuesday, and on and on in the cycle-of-living lifestyle. So much so, that Christ fits naturally into the regular conversation and lifestyle of the home.

GROWING WISE IN FAMILY LIFE, P. 42

*Clothe yourselves with the Lord Jesus Christ.*

ROMANS 13:14 NIV

# FEBRUARY 29

Nothing could ever destroy the Church. It's a permanent building process that will never be crippled by some outside force, never be rendered obsolete, and never be stopped by any power, person, or plan. Period!

GROWING DEEP IN THE CHRISTIAN LIFE, P. 338

*I will build my church; and the gates of hell shall not prevail against it.*

MATTHEW 16:18 KJV

NOVEMBER 2

The third member of the Godhead, the invisible, yet all-powerful representation of deity, is actually living inside your being. The Holy Spirit's limitless capabilities are resident within you, since He indwells you.

GROWING DEEP IN THE CHRISTIAN LIFE, p. 180

*Do you not know that you are the temple of God, and that the Spirit of God dwells in you?*

1 CORINTHIANS 3:16 NKJV

MARCH 1

# May God be praised for the genius of marriage and the thrill of celebrating it annually with the one I love.

GROWING STRONG IN THE SEASONS OF LIFE, P. 329

*Many waters cannot quench love; rivers cannot wash it away.*
*If one were to give all the wealth of his house for love,*
*it would be utterly scorned.*

SONG OF SONGS 8:7 NIV

# NOVEMBER 1

**W**hen God is ready to change a
heart, it gets changed. No one is an
"impossible case" to God. Not even you!

GROWING DEEP IN THE CHRISTIAN LIFE, PP. 154-155

*This is good, and pleases God our Savior, who wants all men
to be saved and to come to a knowledge of the truth.*

1 TIMOTHY 2:3,4 NIV

# MARCH 2

I wait for the truth of Your Word to come to pass, Lord. I wait for help to return. I wait for the promises to become a reality. I wait for the wisdom to take shape and to make sense in my life.

GROWING DEEP IN THE CHRISTIAN LIFE, P. 56

*I wait for the Lord, my soul waits, and in his word I hope.*

PSALM 130:5 NRSV

OCTOBER 31

If your family is still intact, if you're still very much in love, if you're still communicating, still supportive, still laughing and playing together, you're an exception rather than the rule. Our tired, tragic society needs you.

GROWING WISE IN FAMILY LIFE, P. 21

*How good and pleasant it is when brothers live together in unity!*

PSALM 133:1 NIV

MARCH 3

Our Lord often calls His church His bride. Like a bride of beauty and purity in no other color than white, all Christians represent that they are pure, "spiritual" virgins awaiting the joys and intimacies of heavenly marriage with their Groom.

GROWING DEEP IN THE CHRISTIAN LIFE, PP. 289-290

*And to present her to himself as a radiant church, without stain or wrinkle or any other blemish, but holy and blameless.*

EPHESIANS 5:27 NIV

OCTOBER 30

The secret of escape from the prison of this body and the pain of this planet is knowing the One who can guarantee our getting beyond the grave.

GROWING DEEP IN THE CHRISTIAN LIFE, P. 277

*This is eternal life: that they may know you, the only true God, and Jesus Christ, whom you have sent.*

JOHN 17:3 NIV

MARCH 4

Our greatest need is fresh insight from our ever relevant Lord, whose Word is still unsurpassed as a source document of reliable counsel in any generation.

GROWING WISE IN FAMILY LIFE, P. 13

*The word of God is living and active, sharper than any two-edged sword... it is able to judge the thoughts and intentions of the heart.*

HEBREWS 4:12 NRSV

# OCTOBER 29

By returning to our roots, we can become like that tree the psalmist mentions. It is a strong, stable tree, firmly planted by streams of water—one that yields seasonal fruit and has no withering leaves—one that stands the test of time reaching full and enviable maturity.

GROWING DEEP IN THE CHRISTIAN LIFE, p. 408

*His delight is in the law of the Lord, and on his law he meditates day and night. He is like a tree planted by streams of water, which yields its fruit in season and whose leaf does not wither. Whatever he does prospers.*

PSALM 1:2,3 NIV

MARCH 5

We were given to one another by the Lord of the Body—because each one of us has a unique something to contribute—a piece of the divine puzzle no one else on earth can supply.

COME BEFORE WINTER, P. 223

*Just as each of us has one body with many members, and these members do not all have the same function, so in Christ we who are many form one body, and each member belongs to all the others.*

ROMANS 12:4,5 NIV

OCTOBER 28

Generally speaking, there are two kinds of tests in life: adversity and prosperity. Of the two, the latter is the more difficult.

RISE AND SHINE, p. 194

*For the love of money is a root of all kinds of evil, for which some have strayed from the faith in their greediness, and pierced themselves through with many sorrows.*

1 TIMOTHY 6:10 NKJV

MARCH 6

Vision. It is essential for survival. It is spawned by faith, sustained by hope, sparked by imagination and strengthened by enthusiasm. It is greater than sight, deeper than a dream, broader than an idea.

THE QUEST FOR CHARACTER, P. 98

*Now there is in store for me the crown of righteousness, which the Lord, the righteous Judge, will award to me on that day—and not only to me, but also to all who have longed for his appearing.*

2 TIMOTHY 4:8 NIV

OCTOBER 27

God wants our arms around Him. God wants to hear us say, "I love You, Father. I trust You. Whatever You want to give me I accept. I need You. I cling to You. I walk with You. I adore You."

GROWING DEEP IN THE CHRISTIAN LIFE, p. 116

*Love the Lord your God with all your heart and with all your soul and with all your mind and with all your strength.*

MARK 12:30 NIV

MARCH 7

Thoughts, positive or negative, grow stronger
when fertilized with constant repetition.

COME BEFORE WINTER, P. 239

*Casting down imaginations, and every high thing that exalteth
itself against the knowledge of God, and bringing into captivity
every thought to the obedience of Christ.*

2 CORINTHIANS 10:5 KJV

OCTOBER 26

Today—that special block of time holding the key that locks out yesterday's nightmares and unlocks tomorrow's dreams.

THE QUEST FOR CHARACTER, P. 75

*Be very careful, then, how you live—not as unwise but as wise, making the most of every opportunity, because the days are evil.*

EPHESIANS 5:15,16 NIV

# MARCH 8

There will never be a day when God will come back on the scene and say, "You know, I've been rethinking My Book. Some of those truths I wrote about Jesus, well, I need to rewrite all that. Also, a few of the character traits about Me and some of those doctrines in My Book need to be updated."

RISE AND SHINE, P. 138

*Your word, O Lord, is eternal; it stands firm in the heavens.*

PSALM 119:89 NIV

OCTOBER 25

If you must become overinvolved—
become overinvolved in your role as a
character builder in the home.

COME BEFORE WINTER, P. 310

*Train up a child in the way he should go: and
when he is old, he will not depart from it.*

PROVERBS 22:6 KJV

# MARCH 9

# Jesus conceals His surprises until we follow His leading.

THE QUEST FOR CHARACTER, P. 197

*Let us not become weary in doing good, for at the proper time we will reap a harvest if we do not give up.*

GALATIANS 6:9 NIV

# OCTOBER 24

You can remember names. The secret lies in that very brief period of time we stand face-to-face with another person. One of the keys that unlocks a person's soul is his realization that you are interested enough in him to call him by name!

COME BEFORE WINTER, pp. 68-69

*I hope to see you soon, and we will talk face to face. Peace to you. The friends here send their greetings. Greet the friends there by name.*

3 JOHN 14 NIV

# MARCH 10

God still looks out across a wide world and weeps over men and women and children who do not know—have never heard—His healing, life-giving Name.

COME BEFORE WINTER, P. 205

*We have not brought salvation to the earth;*
*we have not given birth to people of the world.*

ISAIAH 26:18 NIV

OCTOBER 23

In worship, there is no place that is free from God's touch. Resistance pushes Him away. And so worship is a response— an active, open, unguarded response to God, whereby we declare His worth in an intimate manner, leaving Him room to touch us, to flood us with His peaceful presence.

GROWING DEEP IN THE CHRISTIAN LIFE, P. 397

*You are my hiding place; you will protect me from trouble and surround me with songs of deliverance.*

PSALM 32:7 NIV

# MARCH 11

Christ doesn't offer a technique on rebuilding
your life. He offers you His life—
His honesty, His integrity.

THE QUEST FOR CHARACTER, PP. 71-72

*Christ in you, the hope of glory.*

COLOSSIANS 1:27 KJV

OCTOBER 22

Rise and shine, friend. Everyone you meet today
is on heaven's Most Wanted List.

RISE & SHINE, P. 71

*Suppose one of you has a hundred sheep and loses one of them.
Does he not leave the ninety-nine in the open country and
go after the lost sheep until he finds it?*

LUKE 15:4 NIV

# MARCH 12

There is a bond deep within that binds us to one another. It is the glue of authentic love, expressing itself in compassion, fairness, willingness to support and, when possible, coming to the aid of another. Personally. Without strings attached.

COME BEFORE WINTER, P. 42

*Love never fails.*

1 CORINTHIANS 13:8 NIV

# OCTOBER 21

The quest for character requires that certain things be kept in the heart as well as kept from the heart. An unguarded heart spells disaster.

THE QUEST FOR CHARACTER, P. 19-20

*Above all else, guard your heart, for it is the wellspring of life.*

PROVERBS 4:23 NIV

MARCH 13

Next to having a good conscience, health is to be valued most. But it isn't! Of all the good and perfect gifts God grants us, it is the least recognized. Mistreated and misunderstood, it exists without encouragement and serves us without reward.

GROWING STRONG IN THE SEASONS OF LIFE, P. 493

*Beloved, I pray that all may go well with you and that you may be in good health, just as it is well with your soul.*

3 JOHN 2 NRSV

OCTOBER 20

It helps me if I remember that God is in charge
of my day—not I.

GROWING STRONG IN THE SEASONS OF LIFE, P. 244

*The steps of a good man are ordered by the Lord:*
*and he delighteth in his way.*

PSALM 37:23 KJV

# MARCH 14

The depth of a church is determined by its quality of worship and instruction. The breadth of a church is determined by its commitment to fellowship and evangelism.

RISE AND SHINE, P. 70

*Every day they continued to meet together in the temple courts. They broke bread in their homes and ate together with glad and sincere hearts.*

ACTS 2:46 NIV

OCTOBER 19

**W**hy not meet your secret longing head on? Why not declare that it's there in your thoughts, waiting for an honest, wise, and intelligent response?

GROWING STRONG IN THE SEASONS OF LIFE, P. 280

*Hope deferred makes the heart sick, but a longing fulfilled is a tree of life.*

PROVERBS 13:12 NIV

MARCH 15

You have available to you the power that's necessary to solve the real problems of your life. He is Jesus Christ.

STRESS FRACTURES, P. 115

*And then shall they see the Son of man coming in the clouds with great power and glory.*

MARK 13:26 KJV

OCTOBER 18

Do you realize there are only two eternal things on earth today? Only two: people and God's Word. Everything else will ultimately be burned up—everything else. Kind of sets your priorities straight, doesn't it?

GROWING DEEP IN THE CHRISTIAN LIFE, P. 61

*The world and its desires pass away, but the man who does the will of God lives forever.*

1 JOHN 2:17 NIV

# MARCH 16

Peace is the ability to stay calm in spite of the panic of unpleasant circumstances.

STRESS FRACTURES, P. 45

*Have mercy on me, O God...for in you my soul takes refuge.*
*I will take refuge in the shadow of your wings*
*until the disaster has passed.*

PSALM 57:1 NIV

OCTOBER 17

$A$s we incorporate leisure into the mainstream
of our world, we lift ourselves above the grit
and grind of mere existence.

STRESS FRACTURES, p. 159

*The thief comes only to steal and kill and destroy; I have come
that they may have life, and have it to the full.*

JOHN 10:10 NIV

MARCH 17

Stationed in the Orient for over a year, I was suddenly faced with sexual temptation as I had never known it. Today I can speak from experience: Sexual abstention works. It pays rich and rewarding dividends.

STRESS FRACTURES, PP. 108-109

*May my heart be blameless toward your decrees,*
*that I may not be put to shame.*

PSALM 119:80 NIV

OCTOBER 16

Regardless of the need, God comforts. He is the God of all comfort! That's His specialty.

FOR THOSE WHO HURT

*Blessed be God, even the Father of our Lord Jesus Christ, the Father of mercies, and the God of all comfort.*

2 CORINTHIANS 1:3 KJV

MARCH 18

It won't be long before you will look back on that up-tight, high-powered, super-charged issue with a whole new outlook. To be quite candid, you may laugh out loud in the future at something you're eating your heart out over today.

GROWING STRONG IN THE SEASONS OF LIFE, P. 42

*You will surely forget your trouble, recalling it only as waters gone by. Life will be brighter than noonday, and darkness will become like morning.*

JOB 11:16,17 NIV

OCTOBER 15

God wants us to know and to do His will; therefore, He is actively engaged in the process of revealing it.

STRESS FRACTURES, P. 231

*Do not conform any longer to the pattern of this world, but be transformed by the renewing of your mind. Then you will be able to test and approve what God's will is—his good, pleasing and perfect will.*

ROMANS 12:2 NIV

MARCH 19

Easter is God's annual question. All across the world on Easter Sunday morning Christ will lean forward and shout, "Do you know where you are going?"

GROWING STRONG IN THE SEASONS OF LIFE, P. 208

*There is a way that seems right to a man, but in the end it leads to death.*

PROVERBS 14:12 NIV

OCTOBER 14

Stumblers who give up are a dime a dozen. In fact, they're useless. Stumblers who get up are as rare as rubies. In fact, they're priceless.

GROWING STRONG IN THE SEASONS OF LIFE, P. 253

*Not that I have already obtained all this, or have already been made perfect, but I press on to take hold of that for which Christ Jesus took hold of me.*

PHILIPPIANS 3:12 NIV

MARCH 20

There is only one YOU. Everything about you is found in only one individual since man first began—YOU.

GROWING STRONG IN THE SEASONS OF LIFE, P. 158

*You created my inmost being; you knit me together in my mother's womb.*

PSALM 139:13 NIV

OCTOBER 13

Crisis crushes. And in crushing, it often refines and purifies. You may be discouraged today because the crushing has not yet led to a surrender. After crises crush sufficiently, God steps in to comfort and teach.

GROWING STRONG IN THE SEASONS OF LIFE, PP. 404-405

*Before I was afflicted I went astray: but now have I kept thy word.*

PSALM 119:67 KJV

# MARCH 21

To stumble is normal—a fact of life—an act that guarantees our humanness. Brush off the dirt with the promise of God's forgiveness—and move on.

GROWING STRONG IN THE SEASONS OF LIFE, P. 252

*We all stumble in many ways. If anyone is never at fault in what he says, he is a perfect man, able to keep his whole body in check.*

JAMES 3:2 NIV

# OCTOBER 12

Don't hide a thing. Show God all those hurts.
He's ready to heal every one—if you're
ready to run toward tomorrow.

COME BEFORE WINTER, P. 142

*Come, and let us return to the Lord; for He has torn, but
He will heal us; He has stricken, but He will bind us up.*

HOSEA 6:1 NKJV

# MARCH 22

The Lord doesn't promise to give us something to take [as a prescription] so we can handle our weary moments. He promises us himself. That is all. And that is enough.

GROWING STRONG IN THE SEASONS OF LIFE, P. 203

*They that wait upon the Lord shall renew their strength; they shall mount up with wings as eagles; they shall run, and not be weary; and they shall walk, and not faint.*

ISAIAH 40:31 KJV

OCTOBER 11

God designed you to be a unique, distinct, significant person unlike any other individual on the face of the earth, throughout the vast expanse of time. The mold was broken, never to be used again, once you entered the flow of mankind.

GROWING STRONG IN THE SEASONS OF LIFE, p. 158

*I will praise You, for I am fearfully and wonderfully made: marvelous are Your works, and that my soul knows very well.*

PSALM 139:14 NKJV

# MARCH 23

**W**here are you? Start there. Openly and freely declare your need to the One who cares deeply.

COME BEFORE WINTER, P. 142

*When I cry unto thee, then shall mine enemies turn back: this I know; for God is for me.*

PSALM 56:9 KJV

OCTOBER 10

It is very important that you understand heaven, our eternal destiny, is an actual place. It isn't a misty dream or a floating fantasy. Don't let any of the mystical religions confuse you. Heaven is reality. Literal real estate which Jesus is preparing for His own. Jesus says so.

GROWING DEEP IN THE CHRISTIAN LIFE, p. 271

*In my Father's house are many rooms; if it were not so, I would have told you. I am going there to prepare a place for you.*

JOHN 14:2 NIV

MARCH 24

A balanced man of God sees the Lord as his strength, his refuge, and his shield when things refuse to be resolved.

STRESS FRACTURES, P. 149

*The Lord is my strength and my shield; my heart trusts in him, and I am helped.*

PSALM 28:7 NIV

OCTOBER 9

I know of no one more needed, more valuable, more Christ-like, than the person who is committed to encouragement.

ENCOURAGE ME, p. 85

*We have different gifts, according to the grace given us. If a man's gift is prophesying, let him use it in proportion to his faith.... If it is encouraging, let him encourage.*

ROMANS 12:6,8 NIV

# MARCH 25

Now that the remedy for sin has been provided, all that remains is receiving it—not having every related question answered.

STRESS FRACTURES, P. 181

*Therefore being justified by faith, we have peace with God through our Lord Jesus Christ.*

ROMANS 5:1 KJV

OCTOBER 8

Once you have the Savior, you also have the Holy Spirit. He will come inside not to mock you but to help you— to empower you to overcome temptation.

STRESS FRACTURES, P. 115

*You, however, are controlled not by the sinful nature but by the Spirit, if the Spirit of God lives in you.*

ROMANS 8:9 NIV

MARCH 26

God isn't playing a guessing game with His people. His will for us is neither puzzling nor hidden within some deep, dark cave requiring magical words to let us in on the secret.

STRESS FRACTURES, P. 231

*He reveals the deep things of darkness and brings deep shadows into the light.*

JOB 12:22 NIV

OCTOBER 7

God wants my unreserved love, my unqualified devotion, my undaunted trust.

GROWING STRONG IN THE SEASONS OF LIFE, p. 397

*Though he slay me, yet will I trust in him.*

JOB 13:15 KJV

MARCH 27

To be an imitator of God requires that we come to terms with the value of quietness, slowing down, coming apart from the noise and speed of today's pace [of life].

STRESS FRACTURES, P. 158

*Be still, and know that I am God: I will be exalted among the heathen, I will be exalted in the earth.*

PSALM 46:10 KJV

OCTOBER 6

Currently—during the interval between our new birth and our Lord's sudden appearance—He is guarding us, keeping us, protecting us, securing us, helping us not to stumble.

GROWING STRONG IN THE SEASONS OF LIFE, P. 117

*If the Lord delights in a man's way, he makes his steps firm; though he stumble, he will not fall, for the Lord upholds him with his hand.*

PSALM 37:23,24 NIV

MARCH 28

Doing what you said you would do is simply an issue of integrity. There is no substitute for having the guts to keep your word.

RISE AND SHINE, P. 191

*Let integrity and uprightness preserve me; for I wait on thee.*

PSALM 25:21 KJV

OCTOBER 5

# Our Lord never wastes times of testing.

COME BEFORE WINTER, p. 278

*But he knows the way that I take; when he has tested me,*
*I will come forth as gold.*

JOB 23:10 NIV

# MARCH 29

We cannot be an encouragement if we live our lives in secret caves, pushing people away from us. People out of touch don't encourage others. Encouragement is a face-to-face thing.

GROWING DEEP IN THE CHRISTIAN LIFE, P. 375

*Having many things to write unto you, I would not write with paper and ink: but I trust to come unto you, and speak face to face, that our joy may be full.*

2 JOHN 12 KJV

OCTOBER 4

When the score is added up one day as we stand before our Lord, many of us will wish we'd played a lot more Risk—and a lot less Trivial Pursuit.

COME BEFORE WINTER, P. 205

*No one engaged in warfare entangles himself with the affairs of this life, that he may please him who enlisted him as a soldier.*

2 TIMOTHY 2:4 NKJV

MARCH 30

The spirit with which we handle our conflicts, the attitudes we exhibit while working through the process of reconciliation is crucial.... That is where our Christianity is often hung out to dry.

COME BEFORE WINTER, P. 66

*Brothers, if someone is caught in a sin, you who are spiritual should restore him gently. But watch yourself, or you also may be tempted.*

GALATIANS 6:1 NIV

OCTOBER 3

We don't make the Scriptures relevant, they are relevant. Our job as Christians is to point out how relevant God's Word really is.

RISE AND SHINE, p. 91

*But in your hearts set apart Christ as Lord. Always be prepared to give an answer to everyone who asks you to give the reason for the hope that you have. But do this with gentleness and respect.*

1 PETER 3:15 NIV

# MARCH 31

Do you work behind the scenes, not seen by the public, as you give time to youth or to adults or to children? That is your worship. It will revolutionize your whole concept of Christian service if you begin to think of your involvement as an act of worship.

GROWING DEEP IN THE CHRISTIAN LIFE, P. 401

*Offer your bodies as living sacrifices, holy and pleasing to God— this is your spiritual act of worship.*

ROMANS 12:1 NIV

OCTOBER 2

It is not mere chance or blind fate that determines the sweeping changes that impact every generation. Our sovereign God takes full responsibility. He tells us it is He who effects change. And the good news is this: When changes occur, they are never out of His control!

RISE AND SHINE, P. 129

*He changes the times and the seasons; he removes kings and raises up kings; he gives wisdom to the wise, and knowledge to those who have understanding.*

DANIEL 2:21 NKJV

# APRIL 1

Home is the bottom line of life, the anvil upon which attitudes and convictions are hammered out—the single most influential force in our earthly existence. No price tag can adequately reflect its value.

HOME: WHERE LIFE MAKES UP ITS MIND, P. 5

*From infancy you have known the holy Scriptures, which are able to make you wise for salvation through faith in Christ Jesus.*

2 TIMOTHY 3:15 NIV

OCTOBER 1

There is too little said these days about the value of a broken and contrite heart. The forgiven sinner of today is often one who expects (dare I say demands?) more than he or she should.

RISE AND SHINE, P. 206

*The sacrifices of God are a broken spirit: a broken and a contrite heart, O God, thou wilt not despise.*

PSALM 51:17 KJV

APRIL 2

Effectiveness—sometimes greatness—awaits those who refuse to run scared.

THE QUEST FOR CHARACTER, P. 85

*Put on the full armor of God, so that when the day of evil comes,*
*you may be able to stand your ground, and after you have*
*done everything, to stand.*

EPHESIANS 6:13 NIV

SEPTEMBER 30

Magnificent goals are achievable if...if our spirits
stay happy...if our morale stays high.

THE QUEST FOR CHARACTER, P. 118

*I know that there is nothing better for men than to be happy
and do good while they live.*

ECCLESIASTES 3:12 NIV

# APRIL 3

It's so easy to get attached to idols—good things, inappropriately adored. But when you have Jesus in the center of the room, everything else only junks up the decor.

COME BEFORE WINTER, P. 81

*Since we are surrounded by such a great cloud of witnesses, let us throw off everything that hinders and the sin that so easily entangles, and let us run with perseverance the race marked out for us.*

HEBREWS 12:1 NIV

# SEPTEMBER 29

Sorrow and her grim family of sighs may drop by for a visit, but they won't stay long when they realize faith got there first—and doesn't plan to leave.

COME BEFORE WINTER, P. 330

*Weeping may endure for a night, but joy cometh in the morning.*

PSALM 30:5 KJV

APRIL 4

Only one Person can step into a life and give it happiness even when health fails—and give it peace even when possessions fade—and give it security when savings fly away.

GROWING STRONG IN THE SEASONS OF LIFE, PP. 400-401

*For God, who commanded the light to shine out of darkness, hath shined in our hearts, to give the light of the knowledge of the glory of God in the face of Jesus Christ.*

2 CORINTHIANS 4:6 KJV

SEPTEMBER 28

If you're an eagle at heart, what are you doing on that perch? Do you have any idea how greatly you're needed to soar and explore?

COME BEFORE WINTER, P. 85

*But they that wait upon the Lord shall renew their strength;*
*they shall mount up with wings as eagles; they shall run,*
*and not be weary; and they shall walk, and not faint.*

ISAIAH 40:31 KJV

# APRIL 5

There is no marital problem so great that God cannot solve it. No marriage—no matter how weak or scarred—need end.

STRIKE THE ORIGINAL MATCH, P. 135

*So guard yourself in your spirit, and do not break faith with the wife of your youth.*

MALACHI 2:15 NIV

SEPTEMBER 27

To live without deadlines is to live an inefficient, unorganized life, drifting with the breeze of impulse on the fickle wave of moods. We set deadlines because they help us accomplish the essentials— they discipline our use of time.

GROWING STRONG IN THE SEASONS OF LIFE, P. 521

*He will die for lack of discipline, led astray by his own great folly.*

PROVERBS 5:23 NIV

# APRIL 6

How our Lord cares for His sheep! How He loves us and rescues us! How often He lifts us when we are low and supports us when we are weak!

GROWING STRONG IN THE SEASONS OF LIFE, P. 117

*He tends his flock like a shepherd: He gathers the lambs in his arms and carries them close to his heart; he gently leads those that have young.*

ISAIAH 40:11 NIV

# SEPTEMBER 26

Opportunity is now. Not later. Now. Your contribution, small though it may seem, is unique and altogether yours. Whatever it may be—it becomes that timeless trophy you invest daily.

GROWING STRONG IN THE SEASONS OF LIFE, P. 265

*Now to each one the manifestation of the Spirit is given for the common good.*

1 CORINTHIANS 12:7 NIV

APRIL 7

Few things heal wounded spirits better than the balm of a supportive embrace.

GROWING STRONG IN THE SEASONS OF LIFE, P. 256

*As a mother comforts her child, so will I comfort you.*

ISAIAH 66:13 NIV

# SEPTEMBER 25

Has something taken the sparkle out of your worship?
Probe deeply. Whatever it is that is stealing your joy and
sucking the life out of your worship must be removed.

GROWING DEEP IN THE CHRISTIAN LIFE, P. 403

*Create in me a clean heart, O God, and put a new and right spirit
within me.... Restore to me the joy of your salvation.*

PSALM 51:6,7,12 NRSV

APRIL 8

If you live intimidated by people, then you need to come to terms with your lack of peace. God is bigger than any person. Learn to focus on people through the lens of God's eye, and you'll never see anyone even near His match.

STRESS FRACTURES, P. 47

*By faith Moses left Egypt, not fearing the king's anger;*
*he persevered because he saw him who is invisible.*

HEBREWS 11:27 NIV

SEPTEMBER 24

Jesus' return will be the absolute greatest surprise. Well, maybe I had better not say that. The greatest surprise is that people like us will be included in the group. That'll be a flat-out miracle.

GROWING STRONG IN THE SEASONS OF LIFE, P. 306

*My offenses will be sealed up in a bag; you will cover over my sin.*

JOB 14:17 NIV

# APRIL 9

Holy Father in Heaven, Your power provides us with hope—hope to start anew, even though we have failed; hope to walk in moral purity, even though we are weak. Amen.

STRESS FRACTURES, P. 116

*For the grace of God that brings salvation has appeared to all men. It teaches us to say "No" to ungodliness and worldly passions, and to live self-controlled, upright and godly lives in this present age.*

TITUS 2:11,12 NIV

SEPTEMBER 23

Nothing enters your life accidentally;
remember that. Behind our every experience
is our loving, sovereign God.

FOR THOSE WHO HURT

*And the Lord will guide you continually, and satisfy your needs...*
*and you shall be like a watered garden, like a spring of water,*
*whose waters never fail.*

ISAIAH 58:11 NRSV

APRIL 10

You were prescribed and then presented to this world exactly as God arranged it.

GROWING STRONG IN THE SEASONS OF LIFE, P. 159

*My frame was not hidden from you when I was made in the secret place. When I was woven together in the depths of the earth, your eyes saw my unformed body.*

PSALM 139:15,16 NIV

# SEPTEMBER 22

# I cannot be the man I should be without times of quietness.

GROWING STRONG IN THE SEASONS OF LIFE, P. 120

*In returning and rest shall ye be saved; in quietness and in confidence shall be your strength.*

ISAIAH 30:15 KJV

APRIL 11

How magnificent is grace! How malignant is guilt! How sweet are the promises! How sour is the past! How precious and broad is God's love! How petty and narrow are man's limitations! How refreshing is the Lord!

GROWING STRONG IN THE SEASONS OF LIFE, P. 374

*I will refresh the weary and satisfy the faint.*

JEREMIAH 31:25 NIV

SEPTEMBER 21

At the cross, when Christ Jesus died,
He "disarmed" all creatures of darkness.
Be strong in the strength of the Champion.

STRESS FRACTURES, P. 197

*And having disarmed the powers and authorities, he made a*
*public spectacle of them, triumphing over them by the cross.*

COLOSSIANS 2:15 NIV

APRIL 12

$\mathsf{T}$he files of heaven are filled with stories of redeemed, refitted renegades and rebels.

GROWING STRONG IN THE SEASONS OF LIFE, P. 373

*Blessed is the man whom God corrects; so do not despise the discipline of the Almighty.*

JOB 5:17 NIV

# SEPTEMBER 20

God's desired will calls for a human response.

STRESS FRACTURES, P. 238

*But if...you seek the Lord your God, you will find him if you look*
*for him with all your heart and with all your soul.*

DEUTERONOMY 4:29 NIV

APRIL 13

Take time to be tender. Fragile and delicate are the feelings of most who seek our help. They need to sense we are there because we care— not just because it's our job.

GROWING STRONG IN THE SEASONS OF LIFE, PP. 352-353

*But we were gentle among you, like a mother caring for her little children.*

1 THESSALONIANS 2:7 NIV

# SEPTEMBER 19

Let your minister be who he is—real. Let him be! Give him the latitude you want for yourself. Give him the same amount of room the grace of God affords you. Don't force him into some traditionalistic mold.

RISE AND SHINE, PP. 235-236

*Welcome him in the Lord with great joy, and honor men like him.*

PHILIPPIANS 2:29 NIV

# APRIL 14

Life is literally filled with God-appointed storms. The massive blows and shattering blasts—not to mention the little, constant irritations—smooth us, humble us, and compel us to submit to His script and His chosen role for our lives.

STARTING OVER, P. 34

*The Lord is slow to anger and great in power; the Lord will not leave the guilty unpunished. His way is in the whirlwind and the storm, and clouds are the dust of his feet.*

NAHUM 1:3 NIV

# SEPTEMBER 18

O Lord. Reassure us that You are our light, our protection, and our shield. We need those reminders. Give them to us each day. May we stand firm in Your power as we find our strength in You, rather than tremble before the enemy. Only through the blood of our Lord Jesus Christ do we conquer! Amen.

STRESS FRACTURES, P. 210

*And hope does not disappoint us, because God has poured out his love into our hearts by the Holy Spirit, whom he has given us.*

ROMANS 5:5 NIV

APRIL 15

Not many really creative people—in the process of creating—keep everything neat, picked up, and in its place.

STRESS FRACTURES, P. 161

*There is a time for everything, and a season for every activity under heaven.... A time to scatter stones and a time to gather them.*

ECCLESIASTES 3:1,5 NIV

SEPTEMBER 17

We are more than conquerors, rather than helpless victims, when it comes to dealing with Satan and his demons.

STRESS FRACTURES, P. 194

*Yet in all these things we are more than conquerors through him who loved us.*

ROMANS 8:37 NKJV

# APRIL 16

I am to trust in my Lord without hesitation and without reservation—with all my heart—so that He might step in and take control, making my way meaningful and straight.

STRESS FRACTURES, P. 20

*Trust in the Lord with all your heart and lean not on your own understanding; in all your ways acknowledge him, and he will make your paths straight.*

PROVERBS 3:5,6 NIV

SEPTEMBER 16

There is nothing about you more magnetic
or attractive than your smile.

ENCOURAGE ME, P. 70

*A glad heart makes a cheerful countenance.*

PROVERBS 15:13 NRSV

APRIL 17

Heaven will be a place of beauty, peace, constant health, and happiness.

STRESS FRACTURES, P. 186

*God shall wipe away all tears from their eyes; and there shall be no more death, neither sorrow, nor crying, neither shall there be any more pain: for the former things are passed away.*

REVELATION 21:4 KJV

SEPTEMBER 15

# When will we learn that God cannot lose?

STRESS FRACTURES, P. 50

*There is no wisdom, no insight, no plan that
can succeed against the Lord.*

PROVERBS 21:30 NIV

# APRIL 18

Our Father is preparing us to meet the deep inner needs of others by bringing us through the dark places first.

FOR THOSE WHO HURT

*God...comforts us in all our troubles, so that we can comfort those in any trouble with the comfort we ourselves have received from God.*

2 CORINTHIANS 1:3,4 NIV

SEPTEMBER 14

The stronger the winds, the deeper the roots, and the longer the winds, the more beautiful the tree.

GROWING STRONG IN THE SEASONS OF LIFE, P. 436

*As you have therefore received Christ Jesus the Lord, so walk in him, rooted and built up in Him and established in the faith, as you have been taught, abounding in it with thanksgiving.*

COLOSSIANS 2:6,7 NKJV

APRIL 19

God not only knows and cares—He understands, He is touched, He is moved. Entering into every pulse of anguish, He longs to sustain and deliver us.

GROWING STRONG IN THE SEASONS OF LIFE, P. 210

*Though I walk through the valley of the shadow of death, I will fear no evil: for thou art with me; thy rod and thy staff they comfort me.*

PSALM 23:4 KJV

SEPTEMBER 13

Mark it—when God forgives, He forgets. He is not only willing but pleased to use any vessel—just as long as it is clean today.

GROWING STRONG IN THE SEASONS OF LIFE, P. 374

*As far as the east is from the west, so far hath he removed our transgressions from us.*

PSALM 103:12 KJV

APRIL 20

Contrary to popular opinion, anyone who sincerely seeks God's will can find it.

STRESS FRACTURES, P. 231

*Ask, and it shall be given you; seek, and ye shall find; knock, and it shall be opened unto you.*

MATTHEW 7:7 KJV

SEPTEMBER 12

# God is personally involved in the very days and details of your life.

GROWING STRONG IN THE SEASONS OF LIFE, P. 159

*All the days ordained for me were written in your book before one of them came to be.*

PSALM 139:16 NIV

# APRIL 21

The lost art of the twentieth century is,
in my opinion, meditation.

GROWING STRONG IN THE SEASONS OF LIFE, P. 285

*Do not let this Book of the Law depart from your mouth;*
*meditate on it day and night, so that you may be careful*
*to do everything written in it. Then you will be*
*prosperous and successful.*

JOSHUA 1:8 NIV

SEPTEMBER 11

Pearls are the product of pain—precious, tiny jewels conceived through irritation, born of adversity, nursed by adjustment.

GROWING STRONG IN THE SEASONS OF LIFE, PP. 244-245

*Consider it pure joy, my brothers, whenever you face trials of many kinds, because you know that the testing of your faith develops perseverance. Perseverance must finish its work so that you may be mature and complete, not lacking anything.*

JAMES 1:2-4 NIV

# APRIL 22

$I$ would much prefer to live my life on the sharp, cutting edge of reality than to dream on the soft, phony mattress of fantasy. Reality is the tempered poker that keeps the fires alive—it's the spark that prompts the engine to keep running.

GROWING STRONG IN THE SEASONS OF LIFE, P. 517

*Much dreaming and many words are meaningless.*
*Therefore stand in awe of God.*

ECCLESIASTES 5:7 NIV

SEPTEMBER 10

The Bible doesn't dodge the tough issues. It offers plain, achievable counsel that works. It promises hope, power, and assurance for those who are weary of losing the battle and living with guilt.

STRESS FRACTURES, PP. 117-118

*But [Jesus] answered and said, "It is written, Man shall not live by bread alone, but by every word that proceeds from the mouth of God."*

MATTHEW 4:4 NKJV

APRIL 23

If I'm writing to a "news junkie" who can't leave the headlines alone, let me make an observation. God never intended us to carry the weight of this broken world on our own shoulders. Give the weight and anxiety back to Him.

RISE AND SHINE, P. 145

*I call on the Lord in my distress, and he answers me.*

PSALM 120:1 NIV

SEPTEMBER 9

Right this moment, take that worry that is eating away at you like a rapidly growing cancer and turn it over to Him. Refuse to brood over it any longer! Cast aside doubt and fear and leave it all with Him.

STRESS FRACTURES, P. 23

*You hear, O Lord, the desire of the afflicted;*
*you encourage them, and you listen to their cry.*

PSALM 10:17 NIV

APRIL 24

Let me encourage you to start singing again. Yes, even when you're alone. Add it to your time with God. Get up with a song. Before anything in the day has a chance to squeeze it out of you, express your praise in a song.

GROWING DEEP IN THE CHRISTIAN LIFE, P. 399

*It is a good thing to give thanks unto the Lord, and to sing praises unto thy name, O most High.*

PSALM 92:1 KJV

# SEPTEMBER 8

When we are lonely, we need an understanding friend. Jesus is the One who "sticks closer than a brother." When we are lonely, we need strength to keep putting one foot in front of the other—Jesus is the One "who strengthens me."

GROWING STRONG IN THE SEASONS OF LIFE, P. 211

*There is a friend who sticks closer than a brother.*

PROVERBS 18:24 NIV

# APRIL 25

Think of church like a huddle at a football game:
You and I know that teams don't show up simply to
huddle. They huddle only long enough to know the plays.
Through the week we run the plays. Sunday after
Sunday we return to the huddle and get the plays.

RISE AND SHINE, P. 69

*Prepare God's people for works of service,
so that the body of Christ may be built up.*

EPHESIANS 4:12 NIV

SEPTEMBER 7

There are times we need to tell ourselves,
"Good job!" when we know that is true.

STRESS FRACTURES, P. 163

*And God saw every thing that he had made, and, behold,
it was very good. And the evening and the
morning were the sixth day.*

GENESIS 1:31 KJV

# APRIL 26

**W**here do you go to find enough stillness to rediscover that God is God? Where do you turn when your days and nights start running together?

COME BEFORE WINTER, P. 317

*But Jesus often withdrew to lonely places and prayed.*

LUKE 5:16 NIV

SEPTEMBER 6

Old age is tough, but when you consider the alternative, it isn't that tough.

STRIKE THE ORIGINAL MATCH, P. 179

*Anyone who is among the living has hope.*

ECCLESIASTES 9:4 NIV

APRIL 27

Rue integrity implies you do what is right
when no one is looking or when everyone
is compromising.

RISE AND SHINE, P. 198

*Whatever you do, work at it with all your heart,
as working for the Lord, not for men.*

COLOSSIANS 3:23 NIV

# SEPTEMBER 5

Great accomplishments are often attempted but only occasionally reached.... Those who reach them are usually those who missed many times before.

GROWING STRONG IN THE SEASONS OF LIFE, P. 371

*But let patience have its perfect work, that you may be perfect and complete, lacking nothing.*

JAMES 1:4 NKJV

# APRIL 28

In the tragic storms of life He specializes in calming waves and silencing winds. It'll just shock you sometimes. How can Jesus Christ do such a thing? He is God!

GROWING DEEP IN THE CHRISTIAN LIFE, P. 147

*And they came to him, and awoke him, saying, Master, master, we perish. Then he arose, and rebuked the wind and the raging of the water: and they ceased, and there was a calm.*

LUKE 8:24 KJV

# SEPTEMBER 4

Balanced Christians are realistic, tolerant people, patient with those who disagree.... They uphold the dignity of others, refusing to put them down.

GROWING DEEP IN THE CHRISTIAN LIFE, P. 40

*Do nothing out of selfish ambition or vain conceit, but in humility consider others better than yourselves.*

PHILIPPIANS 2:3 NIV

APRIL 29

I acknowledge the Creator-God as my heavenly Father, infinitely perfect, and intimately acquainted with all my ways.

GROWING DEEP IN THE CHRISTIAN LIFE, P. 15

*Does he not see my ways and count my every step?*

JOB 31:4 NIV

# SEPTEMBER 3

# You and I become what we think about.

COME BEFORE WINTER, P. 238

*For as he thinketh in his heart, so is he.*

PROVERBS 23:7 KJV

# APRIL 30

Discouraged people don't need critics. They hurt enough already. They don't need more guilt or piled-on distress. They need encouragement. They need a refuge.

GROWING STRONG IN THE SEASONS OF LIFE, P. 380

*The Lord also will be a refuge for the oppressed,*
*a refuge in times of trouble.*

PSALM 9:9 KJV

# SEPTEMBER 2

# Don't weary yourself trying to unscrew the inscrutable.

GROWING DEEP IN THE CHRISTIAN LIFE, P. 101

*The secret things belong to the Lord our God, but the things revealed belong to us and to our children forever, that we may follow all the words of this law.*

DEUTERONOMY 29:29 NIV

# MAY 1

Ht gives me a growing sense of inner peace to remember that God's chapters are still being written. He has not yet said, "The end."

RISE AND SHINE, P. 158

*Because of the Lord's great love we are not consumed, for his compassions never fail. They are new every morning; great is your faithfulness.*

LAMENTATIONS 3:22,23 NIV

SEPTEMBER 1

Being in Christ is the safest place in life. And in calamity. And in death. In Him, and in Him alone, we are secure. Eternally secure.

STRESS FRACTURES, P. 268

*Who shall separate us from the love of Christ? Shall trouble or hardship or persecution or famine or nakedness or danger or sword?... No, in all these things we are more than conquerors through him who loved us.*

ROMANS 8:35,37 NIV

MAY 2

A great lover is someone who can satisfy one woman all her life long—and who can be satisfied by one woman all his life long.

STRIKE THE ORIGINAL MATCH, P. 27

*Place me like a seal over your heart, like a seal on your arm;*
*for love is as strong as death, its jealousy unyielding as the grave.*
*It burns like blazing fire, like a mighty flame.*

SONG OF SONGS 8:6 NIV

AUGUST 31

God has given each of us the Bible in our tongue. Each one of us has the potential to become adequate, mature, equipped for every good work.

RISE AND SHINE, PP. 177-178

*All Scripture is God-breathed and is useful for teaching, rebuking, correcting and training in righteousness, so that the man of God may be thoroughly equipped for every good work.*

2 TIMOTHY 3:16,17 NIV

MAY 3

I need a faith that nothing can shake. Emphasis on NOTHING. Even when I do not know why, I can endure with a faith like that—even if I never find out why!

GROWING WISE IN FAMILY LIFE, P. 247

*Be strong and courageous...for the Lord your God goes with you;*
*he will never leave you nor forsake you.*

DEUTERONOMY 31:6 NIV

# AUGUST 30

# The way to stop a loud argument is by a soft-spoken word.

COME BEFORE WINTER, P. 303

*A soft answer turneth away wrath:*
*but grievous words stir up anger.*

PROVERBS 15:1 KJV

MAY 4

Trust in no substitutes, seek no other refuge, lean on no other crutch but the living God. Love Him as you love no one else on earth.

GROWING DEEP IN THE CHRISTIAN LIFE, P. 109

*Whom have I in heaven but you? And there is nothing on earth that I desire other than you.*

PSALM 73:25 NRSV

AUGUST 29

Death brings sorrow. Sorrow brings tears. Tears are part of the grieving process. God never tells us, "Don't cry. Don't grieve." He says we are not to grieve as those who have no hope.

GROWING DEEP IN THE CHRISTIAN LIFE, P. 275

*Brothers, we do not want you to be ignorant about those who fall asleep, or to grieve like the rest of men, who have no hope. We believe that Jesus died and rose again and so we believe that God will bring with Jesus those who have fallen asleep in him.*

1 THESSALONIANS 4:13,14 NIV

# MAY 5

God knows what He's about. If He has you sidelined, out of the action for a while, He knows what He's doing. You just stay faithful—stay flexible—stay available—stay humble.

GROWING STRONG IN THE SEASONS OF LIFE, P. 531

*Commit thy way unto the Lord; trust also in him;*
*and he shall bring it to pass.*

PSALM 37:5 KJV

# AUGUST 28

# Nothing needs to be watched more closely than credit buying.

STRIKE THE ORIGINAL MATCH, P. 130

*The rich rule over the poor, and the borrower is servant to the lender.*

PROVERBS 22:7 NIV

MAY 6

Love. No greater theme can be emphasized.
No stronger message can be proclaimed.
No finer song can be sung.
No better truth can be imagined.

THE QUEST FOR CHARACTER, P. 181

*The Lord is gracious and compassionate, slow to anger and rich in love.*

PSALM 145:8 NIV

AUGUST 27

The unusual is God's standard procedure. The Bible is full of individuals and families who broke the mold of the predictable as they accomplished the incredible.

GROWING WISE IN FAMILY LIFE, P. 266

*By faith Abraham, even though he was past age—and Sarah herself was barren—was enabled to become a father because he considered him faithful who had made the promise. And so from this one man, and he as good as dead, came descendants as numerous as the stars in the sky and as countless as the sand on the seashore.*

HEBREWS 11:11,12 NIV

MAY 7

God makes His will known: (1) through His Word—as we stop and study it, (2) through circumstances—as we look within and sense what He is saying, and (3) through the counsel of others—as we listen carefully.

STRESS FRACTURES, P. 244

*Be transformed by the renewing of your mind. Then you will be able to test and approve what God's will is.*

ROMANS 12:2 NIV

AUGUST 26

Turn your Goliath over to Jehovah, the giant-killer.
Explain to your powerful God how anxious you are
for Him to win this victory for a change—
not the giant, and not you.

COME BEFORE WINTER, P. 148

*I am God. Yes, and from ancient days I am he. No one can deliver
out of my hand. When I act, who can reverse it?*

ISAIAH 43:12,13 NIV

MAY 8

Is there some soul known to you in need of financial encouragement? A student off at school—a young couple up against it—a divorcee struggling to gain back self-acceptance—a forgotten servant of God laboring in an obscure and difficult ministry? Encourage generously!

GROWING STRONG IN THE SEASONS OF LIFE, P. 215

*And do not forget to do good and to share with others,*
*for with such sacrifices God is pleased.*

HEBREWS 13:16 NIV

# AUGUST 25

$N$o amount of doctrine will replace our need for encouraging relationships built on love and understanding. Knowledge may strengthen, but relationships soften. A healthy church family has both.

GROWING DEEP IN THE CHRISTIAN LIFE, P. 388

*If one part suffers, every part suffers with it; if one part is honored, every part rejoices with it.*

1 CORINTHIANS 12:26 NIV

MAY 9

# Prayer is an essential therapy during stressful times.

STRESS FRACTURES, P. 27

*David was greatly distressed, for the people spoke of stoning him....*
*But David strengthened himself in the Lord his God.*

1 SAMUEL 30:6 NKJV

# AUGUST 24

Big problems frequently strengthen marriages.
It's the little things we seldom even consider
that cut away at the heart of a home.

STRIKE THE ORIGINAL MATCH, P. 87

*Catch for us the foxes, the little foxes that ruin the vineyards.*

SONG OF SONGS 2:15 NIV

MAY 10

Are you facing some difficult battle today? Don't run! Stand still and refuse to retreat. Look at it as God looks at it and draw upon His power to hold up under the blast.

COME BEFORE WINTER, P. 181

*Thus says the Lord to you, "Do not fear or be dismayed at this great multitude; for the battle is not yours, but God's."*

2 CHRONICLES 20:15 NRSV

# AUGUST 23

How does glorifying God occur? By cultivating the habit of including the Lord God in every segment of your life. By refusing to expect or accept any of the glory that belongs to God. By maintaining a priority relationship with Him that is more important than any other on earth.

RISE AND SHINE, PP. 29-31

*I will praise you, O Lord my God, with all my heart;*
*I will glorify your name forever.*

PSALM 86:12 NIV

# MAY 11

Nobodies...exalting Somebody. Are you one? Listen to me! It's the "nobodies" Somebody chooses so carefully. And when He has selected you for that role, He does not consider you a nobody.

GROWING STRONG IN THE SEASONS OF LIFE, P. 129

*But God has combined the members of the body and has given greater honor to the parts that lacked it.*

1 CORINTHIANS 12:24 NIV

AUGUST 22

You need someone and someone needs you. To make this thing called life work, we have to lean and support. And relate and respond. And give and take. And confess and forgive. And reach out and embrace.

COME BEFORE WINTER, P. 116

*Two are better than one; because they have a good reward for their labour.*

ECCLESIASTES 4:9 KJV

MAY 12

I have tried and I cannot find, either in Scripture or history, a strong-willed individual whom God used greatly, until He allowed him to be hurt deeply.

COME BEFORE WINTER, P. 152

*Just as the sufferings of Christ flow over into our lives,*
*so also through Christ our comfort overflows.*

2 CORINTHIANS 1:5 NIV

AUGUST 21

# Never forget, we're the ones who belong to the King.

GROWING STRONG IN THE SEASONS OF LIFE, P. 219

*What shall we then say to these things?*
*If God be for us, who can be against us?*

ROMANS 8:31 KJV

# MAY 13

This hope Christ can bring, this "anchor of the soul," is the only way through. I have no answer other than Jesus Christ.

STRESS FRACTURES, P. 229

*We have this hope as an anchor for the soul, firm and secure. It enters the inner sanctuary behind the curtain, where Jesus, who went before us, has entered on our behalf.*

HEBREWS 6:19,20 NIV

# AUGUST 20

Did you blow it this week? So did I! Satan smiles smugly when we get discouraged and throw in the towel. Let's not give him that satisfaction. Knowing how our enemy hates love and forgiveness, let's give those very things to ourselves and others—starting today.

GROWING STRONG IN THE SEASONS OF LIFE, P. 381

*His divine power has given us everything we need for life and godliness through our knowledge of him who called us by his own glory and goodness.*

2 PETER 1:3 NIV

MAY 14

W e've been programmed to think that
fatigue is next to godliness.

STRESS FRACTURES, P. 157

*In vain you rise early and stay up late, toiling for food to eat—*
*for he grants sleep to those he loves.*

PSALM 127:2 NIV

AUGUST 19

Doubt says, "You fool, you're stupid to believe in a God who put you through this." By faith, keep remembering that God cannot lie.

STRESS FRACTURES, P. 226

*Lift up your eyes to the heavens, look at the earth beneath; the heavens will vanish like smoke, the earth will wear out like a garment.... But my salvation will last forever, my righteousness will never fail.*

ISAIAH 51:6 NIV

MAY 15

Think of the Bible as the absolutely reliable instrument panel designed to get people, and to keep people, on the right track.

STRESS FRACTURES, P. 177

*Your word is a lamp to my feet and a light for my path.*

PSALM 119:105 NIV

AUGUST 18

God wants to use you—stumbling and all.
But He won't do so if you refuse to get up.

STARTING OVER, P. 7

*Then Jesus said to him, "Get up! Pick up your mat and walk."*

JOHN 5:8 NIV

MAY 16

Your Savior knows your breaking point. The bruising
and crushing and melting process is designed to
reshape you, not ruin you. Your value is increasing
the longer He lingers over you.

ENCOURAGE ME, P. 36

*For he wounds, but he also binds up; he injures, but his hands also heal.*

JOB 5:18 NIV

AUGUST 17

The only thing we can be thankful for when it comes to blowing it is that nobody keeps a record. Or do they? Or do you with others? Not if you are serious about encouragement. Come on, ease off.

ENCOURAGE ME, P. 67

*Be kind one to another, tenderhearted, forgiving one another, as God in Christ has forgiven you.*

EPHESIANS 4:32 NRSV

MAY 17

I wonder how many tear bottles in heaven bear your initials. You'll never have many until you let go and let a little tenderness run loose.

GROWING STRONG IN THE SEASONS OF LIFE, P. 164

*Record my lament; list my tears on your scroll—*
*are they not in your record?*

PSALM 56:8 NIV

# AUGUST 16

I may tremble on the Rock, but the Rock never trembles under me!

STRESS FRACTURES, P. 267

*He alone is my rock and my salvation;*
*he is my fortress, I will never be shaken.*

PSALM 62:2 NIV

MAY 18

I suggest a new watchword for our times.
ENCOURAGEMENT! Shout it out.
Pass it around.

GROWING STRONG IN THE SEASONS OF LIFE, P. 216

*Pleasant words are like a honeycomb,*
*Sweetness to the soul and health to the bones.*

PROVERBS 16:24 NKJV

AUGUST 15

Consistent, timely encouragement has the staggering magnetic power to draw an immortal soul to the God of hope. The One whose name is Wonderful Counselor.

ENCOURAGE ME, P. 85

*For to us a child is born, to us a son is given, and the government will be on his shoulders. And he will be called Wonderful Counselor, Mighty God, Everlasting Father, Prince of Peace.*

ISAIAH 9:6 NIV

MAY 19

Does something seem terribly important to you today? Extremely, vitally serious? Almost to the point of distraction? Number your days. Get a little perspective.

GROWING STRONG IN THE SEASONS OF LIFE, P. 42

*Teach us to number our days aright, that we may gain a heart of wisdom.*

PSALM 90:12 NIV

AUGUST 14

A teardrop on earth summons the King of Heaven.

GROWING STRONG IN THE SEASONS OF LIFE, P. 163

*Even now my witness is in heaven; my advocate is on high.*
*My intercessor is my friend as my eyes pour out tears to God;*
*on behalf of a man he pleads with God as a man pleads for his friend.*

JOB 16:19-21 NIV

MAY 20

If God can take a disobedient prophet [like Jonah], turn him around, and set him on fire spiritually, He can do the same with you.

COME BEFORE WINTER, P. 142

*I, with a song of thanksgiving, will sacrifice to you. What I have vowed I will make good. Salvation comes from the Lord.*

JONAH 2:9 NIV

# AUGUST 13

Extracting the hurtful thorns of habit enables the pilgrim to focus less attention on himself and more attention on the One who is worthy.

GROWING STRONG IN THE SEASONS OF LIFE, P. 83

*I have been crucified with Christ and I no longer live, but Christ lives in me. The life I live in the body, I live by faith in the Son of God, who loved me and gave himself for me.*

GALATIANS 2:20 NIV

MAY 21

**W**hat a beautiful, refreshing thing it would be to see most of God's people relaxing in Him!

STRESS FRACTURES, P. 30

*Anyone who enters God's rest also rests from his own work, just as God did from his.*

HEBREWS 4:10 NIV

# AUGUST 12

The beauty of grace—our only permanent deliverance
from guilt—is that it meets us where we are
and gives us what we don't deserve.

STRESS FRACTURES, P. 264

*Because of his great love for us, God, who is rich in mercy,
made us alive with Christ even when we were dead in
transgressions—it is by grace you have been saved.*

EPHESIANS 2:4,5 NIV

MAY 22

**G**od asks that we believe Him regardless of the
risks—in spite of the danger—ignoring the odds.

GROWING STRONG IN THE SEASONS OF LIFE, P. 370

*By faith Abraham, when God tested him, offered Isaac as a sacrifice. He...
was about to sacrifice his one and only son, even though God had said
to him, "It is through Isaac that your offspring will be reckoned."*

HEBREWS 11:17,18 NIV

# AUGUST 11

If we could see as our Father sees, I'm convinced we would be amazed at the size of His family. If the spiritual iceberg were suddenly turned upside down and exposed for all to view, the magnitude of the Church He is building would literally take our breath away.

GROWING STRONG IN THE SEASONS OF LIFE, P. 218

*I looked and there before me was a great multitude that no one could count, from every nation, tribe, people and language, standing before the throne.*

REVELATION 7:9 NIV

MAY 23

Only one decision pleases God—obedience.

STRESS FRACTURES, P. 102

*Hath the Lord as great delight in burnt offerings and sacrifices,*
*as in obeying the voice of the Lord? Behold, to obey*
*is better than sacrifice.*

1 SAMUEL 15:22 KJV

AUGUST 10

Real truth, truth you can rely on, truth that will never turn sour, that will never backfire, that's the truth in the Bible.

GROWING DEEP IN THE CHRISTIAN LIFE, P. 59

*You are my refuge and my shield;*
*I have put my hope in your word.*

PSALM 119:114 NIV

MAY 24

Your Monday through Friday employment is pure, it's sacred—just as sacred as your Sunday activities.

GROWING STRONG IN THE SEASONS OF LIFE, P. 87

*Whatever you do or say, let it be as a representative of the Lord Jesus.*

COLOSSIANS 3:17 TLB

# AUGUST 9

Changing times require the willingness to retool and flex where needed. Changeless truths require the discipline to resist and fight when necessary.

RISE AND SHINE, PP. 142-143

*Fight the good fight, holding on to faith and a good conscience. Some have rejected these and so have shipwrecked their faith.*

1 TIMOTHY 1:18,19 NIV

MAY 25

Our sole purpose, our basic reason for existence, is to bring maximum glory to our God—to magnify, exalt, and elevate the Lord our God.

RISE AND SHINE, PP. 20, 23

*So whether you eat or drink or whatever you do,*
*do it all for the glory of God.*

1 CORINTHIANS 10:31 NIV

AUGUST 8

God, our wise and creative Maker, has been pleased to make everyone different and no one perfect. The sooner we appreciate and accept that fact, the deeper we will appreciate and accept one another.

GROWING STRONG IN THE SEASONS OF LIFE, P. 416

*Accept him whose faith is weak, without passing judgment on disputable matters.*

ROMANS 14:1 NIV

MAY 26

God's great net of security spans this globe.
No matter where His children live, He has stretched
out His everlasting arms beneath them.

STRESS FRACTURES, P. 268

*The eternal God is thy refuge, and underneath are the everlasting arms.*

DEUTERONOMY 33:27 KJV

# AUGUST 7

# Those who give generously have much more than those who hoard.

COME BEFORE WINTER, P. 303

*Give, and it will be given to you. A good measure, pressed down, shaken together and running over, will be poured into your lap. For with the measure you use, it will be measured to you.*

LUKE 6:38 NIV

MAY 27

We are witnesses and spokesmen for the God of infinite variety, boundless creativity, indescribable majesty and beauty. We hold in our possession a white-hot message of hope, a pulsating invitation to approach a living Savior.

GROWING STRONG IN THE SEASONS OF LIFE, P. 226

*We are therefore Christ's ambassadors, as though God were making his appeal through us. We implore you on Christ's behalf: Be reconciled to God.*

2 CORINTHIANS 5:20 NIV

AUGUST 6

God still desires to impact our generation with remarkable families of faith—that includes you and your family.

GROWING WISE IN FAMILY LIFE, P. 25

*Choose for yourselves this day whom you will serve....*
*But as for me and my house, we will serve the Lord.*

JOSHUA 24:15 NKJV

MAY 28

All Scripture in its original form has been breathed out by God so that a writer, under the controlling power of the Spirit of God, wrote the Scriptures precisely as God would have them written.

RISE AND SHINE, P. 177

*All Scripture is God-breathed and is useful for teaching, rebuking, correcting and training in righteousness.*

2 TIMOTHY 3:16 NIV

AUGUST 5

Though person who succeeds is not the one who holds back, fearing failure, nor the one who never fails—but rather the one who moves on in spite of failure.

GROWING STRONG IN THE SEASONS OF LIFE, P. 370

*Commit to the Lord whatever you do, and your plans will succeed.*

PROVERBS 16:3 NIV

MAY 29

Ask God to open your lips and honor your words—
but be careful! Once your missile hits the target,
you'll become totally dissatisfied with your former
life as an earth-bound, secret service saint.

COME BEFORE WINTER, P. 44

*So is my word that goes out from my mouth: It will not return to me empty,*
*but will accomplish what I desire and achieve the purpose for which I sent it.*

ISAIAH 55:11 NIV

# AUGUST 4

Your mind is a muscle. It needs to be stretched to stay sharp. It needs to be prodded and pushed to perform.

GROWING STRONG IN THE SEASONS OF LIFE, P. 425

*Wise men store up knowledge, but the mouth of a fool invites ruin.*

PROVERBS 10:14 NIV

MAY 30

Filter everything through the same question:
Will this bring glory to God or to me?

RISE AND SHINE, P. 33

*He must become greater; I must become less.*

JOHN 3:30 NIV

AUGUST 3

A marriage is maintained and strengthened
by compromise as is the relationship
between parent and child.

THE QUEST FOR CHARACTER, P. 151

*Though one may be overpowered, two can defend themselves.*
*A cord of three strands is not quickly broken.*

ECCLESIASTES 4:12 NIV

MAY 31

$\int$piritually speaking, the Spirit of God was there
as you were born into God's eternal family,
leading you to say "Abba." You have a "daddy"
relationship with your Father.

GROWING WISE IN FAMILY LIFE, P. 277

*You did not receive a spirit that makes you a slave again to fear, but you
received the Spirit of sonship. And by him we cry, "Abba, Father."*

ROMANS 8:15 NIV

AUGUST 2

Times may be hard and people may be demanding, but never forget that life is special. Every single day is a special day. God is at work in you!

THE QUEST FOR CHARACTER, P. 207

*For it is God who works in you both to will and to do for His good pleasure.*

PHILIPPIANS 2:13 NKJV

JUNE 1

Neither waves nor winds intimidate Him. There is no swell that causes our God to suck in His breath out of fear. There is no depth that causes Him to lift His eyebrows in amazement. He made it all!

GROWING DEEP IN THE CHRISTIAN LIFE, P. 395

*Before the mountains were born or you brought forth the earth and the world, from everlasting to everlasting you are God.*

PSALM 90:2 NIV

# AUGUST 1

God has ordained and established
three great institutions:

The home—"Fill the earth and subdue it."
GENESIS 1:28 NIV

The church—"I will build my church."
MATTHEW 16:18 NIV

The government—"Authorities are God's servants."
ROMANS 13:6 NIV

COME BEFORE WINTER, P. 309

JUNE 2

There is great security in opening God's timeless Book and hearing His voice. It calms our fears. It clears our heads. It comforts our hearts. Let it have its entrance today.

THE QUEST FOR CHARACTER, P. 186

*For everything that was written in the past was written to teach us, so that through endurance and the encouragement of the Scriptures we might have hope.*

ROMANS 15:4 NIV

JULY 31

I know of no realm of life that can provide more companionship in a lonely world or greater feelings of security and purpose in chaotic times than the close ties of a family.

GROWING WISE IN FAMILY LIFE, PP. 291-292

*Your wife shall be like a fruitful vine in the very heart of your house, your children like olive plants all around your table.*

PSALM 128:3 NKJV

JUNE 3

Every time we encourage someone,
we give them a transfusion of courage.

GROWING DEEP IN THE CHRISTIAN LIFE, P. 380

*An anxious heart weighs a man down,
but a kind word cheers him up.*

PROVERBS 12:25 NIV

JULY 30

# You can't trust Satan's cease-fires.

THE QUEST FOR CHARACTER, P. 24

*The thief comes only to steal and kill and destroy; I have come*
*that they may have life, and have it to the full.*

JOHN 10:10 NIV

# JUNE 4

If necessity is the mother of invention,
persistence is certainly the father.

COME BEFORE WINTER, P. 139

*Since through God's mercy we have this ministry,
we do not lose heart.*

2 CORINTHIANS 4:1 NIV

JULY 29

Ⅰf you are one of those seers, a tomorrow-thinker
in a world of yesterday-dwellers, take heart.
Realize that you must be true to yourself.

COME BEFORE WINTER, P. 178

*For we walk by faith, not by sight.*

2 CORINTHIANS 5:7 KJV

JUNE 5

The very best platform upon which we may build a case for Christianity at work rests on six massive pillars: integrity, faithfulness, punctuality, quality workmanship, a pleasant attitude, and enthusiasm.

GROWING STRONG IN THE SEASONS OF LIFE, P. 86

*Let your light so shine before men, that they may see your good works, and glorify your Father which is in heaven.*

MATTHEW 5:16 KJV

JULY 28

We see now. Our Lord sees forever. We judge on the basis of the temporal; He, on the basis of the eternal.

GROWING STRONG IN THE SEASONS OF LIFE, P. 241

*A thousand years in your sight are like a day that has just gone by, or like a watch in the night.*

PSALM 90:4 NIV

JUNE 6

Our only ground of victory over evil powers is our union with the Lord Jesus Christ.

STRESS FRACTURES, P. 205

*I am the vine; you are the branches. If a man remains in me and I in him, he will bear much fruit; apart from me you can do nothing.*

JOHN 15:5 NIV

JULY 27

In worship we become preoccupied with the Lord. We don't watch something happen, we participate in it. One "connects" with the living God. It is almost as though you could reach out and touch Him.

GROWING DEEP IN THE CHRISTIAN LIFE, P. 395

*Exalt ye the Lord our God, and worship at his footstool; for he is holy.*

PSALM 99:5 KJV

JUNE 7

Y‍ou are YOU. There is only one YOU.
And YOU are important.

GROWING STRONG IN THE SEASONS OF LIFE, P. 161

*For you created my inmost being; you knit me together*
*in my mother's womb. I praise you because*
*I am fearfully and wonderfully made.*

PSALM 139:13,14 NIV

# JULY 26

Everyone who enters the world is a person of worth and dignity.

STRESS FRACTURES, P. 136

*So God created man in his own image, in the image of God created he him; male and female created he them.*

GENESIS 1:27 KJV

JUNE 8

Tucked away in a quiet corner of every life are wounds and scars. If they were not there, we would need no Physician. Nor would we need one another.

GROWING STRONG IN THE SEASONS OF LIFE, P. 114

*Be merciful to me, Lord, for I am faint; O Lord, heal me.*

PSALM 6:2 NIV

JULY 25

Today is unique! It has never occurred before and it will never be repeated. At midnight it will end, quietly, suddenly, totally. Forever. But the hours between now and then are opportunities with eternal possibilities.

THE QUEST FOR CHARACTER, P. 191

*For we are God's workmanship, created in Christ Jesus to do good works, which God prepared in advance for us to do.*

EPHESIANS 2:10 NIV

# JUNE 9

Υou don't "fit the mold"? Is that what sent you down into the valley of discouragement? You don't sound like every other Christian or look like the "standard" saint? Hallelujah!

GROWING STRONG IN THE SEASONS OF LIFE, PP. 160-161

*The Lord does not look at the things man looks at. Man looks at the outward appearance, but the Lord looks at the heart."*

1 SAMUEL 16:7 NIV

JULY 24

Τrue fellowship means that we care about
and therefore care for one another.

RISE AND SHINE, P. 49

*I hope to visit you while passing through and to have you assist me
on my journey there, after I have enjoyed your company for a while.*

ROMANS 15:24 NIV

JUNE 10

I'm afraid that some long-faced saints would crack their concrete masks if they smiled—I really am! Nothing repels like a frown—or attracts like a smile.

ENCOURAGE ME, P. 70

*A cheerful look brings joy to the heart, and good news gives health to the bones.*

PROVERBS 15:30 NIV

JULY 23

The Great Commission is still "The Great Commission," not "The Limited Agreement for My Corner of America."

COME BEFORE WINTER, P. 205

*And he said unto them, Go ye into all the world, and preach the gospel to every creature.*

MARK 16:15 KJV

JUNE 11

Peace is the ability to wait patiently in spite
of panic brought on by uncertainty.

STRESS FRACTURES, P. 50

*Peace I leave with you; my peace I give you. I do not give
to you as the world gives. Do not let your hearts
be troubled and do not be afraid.*

JOHN 14:27 NIV

JULY 22

# Greatness and the attention to detail, in my opinion, are welded together.

COME BEFORE WINTER, P. 62

*Do you see a man skilled in his work? He will serve before kings; he will not serve before obscure men.*

PROVERBS 22:29 NIV

JUNE 12

A major portion of our eye troubles could probably be diagnosed "ingrownius eyeballitus." Ingrown eyeballs.

GROWING STRONG IN THE SEASONS OF LIFE, P. 335

*Let us fix our eyes on Jesus, the author and perfecter of our faith, who for the joy set before him endured the cross, scorning its shame, and sat down at the right hand of the throne of God.*

HEBREWS 12:2 NIV

JULY 21

Wise is the listener who doesn't feel compelled
to fill up all the blank spaces.

GROWING STRONG IN THE SEASONS OF LIFE, P. 90

*The hearing ear, and the seeing eye,
the Lord hath made even both of them.*

PROVERBS 20:12 KJV

JUNE 13

God is the One who builds trophies from the scrap pile—who draws His clay from under the bridge—who makes clean instruments of beauty from the filthy failures of yesteryear.

STARTING OVER, P. 23

*You are already clean because of the word I have spoken to you.*

JOHN 15:3 NIV

# JULY 20

Cultivate your own capabilities. Rabbits don't fly. Eagles don't swim. Ducks look funny trying to climb. Squirrels don't have feathers. Stop comparing. Enjoy being you! There's plenty of room in the forest.

GROWING STRONG IN THE SEASONS OF LIFE, P. 464

*We have different gifts, according to the grace given us.*

ROMANS 12:6 NIV

JUNE 14

# It is never too late to start doing what is right!

GROWING DEEP IN THE CHRISTIAN LIFE, P. 380

*Everyone who calls on the name of the Lord will be saved.*

JOEL 2:32 NIV

# JULY 19

The secret of good parenting is consistency.
Never forget that! Stay at it, day in and day out.

GROWING STRONG IN THE SEASONS OF LIFE, P. 394

*Discipline your children, and they will give you rest;*
*they will give delight to your heart.*

PROVERBS 29:17 NRSV

JUNE 15

JUNE 16

When you accept the fact that sometimes seasons are dry and times are hard and that God is in control of both, you will discover a sense of divine refuge, because the hope then is in God and not in yourself.

STRESS FRACTURES, P. 222

*Because God wanted to make the unchanging nature of his purpose very clear...we who have fled to take hold of the hope offered to us may be greatly encouraged.*

HEBREWS 6:17,18 NIV

JULY 17

Confident living is directly linked
to being "unblamable."

STRESS FRACTURES, P. 103

*He will keep you strong to the end, so that you will be
blameless on the day of our Lord Jesus Christ.*

1 CORINTHIANS 1:8 NIV

JUNE 17

**Y**ou can have fun and still be efficient.
In fact, you will be more efficient!

STRESS FRACTURES, P. 155

*The joy of the Lord is your strength.*

NEHEMIAH 8:10 KJV

JULY 16

Encouragement is awesome. It has the capacity to lift a man's or woman's shoulders. To spark the flicker of a smile on the face of a discouraged child. To breathe fresh fire into the fading embers of a smoldering dream. To actually change the course of another human being's day, week, or life.

ENCOURAGE ME, P. 85

*Therefore encourage one another and build each other up, just as in fact you are doing.*

1 THESSALONIANS 5:11 NIV

JUNE 18

Why do we need a refuge? Because we are in distress and sorrow accompanies us. Because we are sinful and guilt accuses us. Because we are surrounded by adversaries and misunderstanding assaults us.

GROWING STRONG IN THE SEASONS OF LIFE, PP. 378-379

*God is our refuge and strength, a very present help in trouble.*

PSALM 46:1 KJV

JULY 15

God is a Specialist at making something useful and beautiful out of something broken and confused.

COME BEFORE WINTER, P. 142

*Before they call I will answer; while they are still speaking I will hear.*

ISAIAH 65:24 NIV

JUNE 19

I think it is often just as sacred to laugh as it is to pray—or preach—or witness.

GROWING STRONG IN THE SEASONS OF LIFE, P. 148

*Our mouths were filled with laughter,*
*our tongues with songs of joy.*

PSALM 126:2 NIV

JULY 14

There is nothing wrong or unnatural with feeling weary,
but there is everything wrong with abandoning ship
in the midst of the fight.

GROWING STRONG IN THE SEASONS OF LIFE, P. 202

*Hear me, O Lord; for thy lovingkindness is good: turn unto me*
*according to the multitude of thy tender mercies.*

PSALM 69:16 KJV

JUNE 20

God's medal-of-honor winners are made in secret
because their most courageous acts occur—
away from the hurricane of public opinion—
up in the attic, hidden from public knowledge.

GROWING STRONG IN THE SEASONS OF LIFE, P. 544

*Your Father, who sees what is done in secret, will reward you.*

MATTHEW 6:4 NIV

JULY 13

Failures are only temporary tests to prepare us for permanent triumphs. Start doing something that you've put off because of the risk of failure.

GROWING STRONG IN THE SEASONS OF LIFE, P. 371

*Now faith is being sure of what we hope for and certain of what we do not see.*

HEBREWS 11:1 NIV

JUNE 21

There will be times a church must be steel, and other times it will have to be velvet. A church that is all steel is harsh and calculating. A church that is all velvet becomes too soft, too tolerant, accepting anything and lacking in conviction.

RISE AND SHINE, P. 91

*We are his house, if we hold on to our courage and the hope of which we boast.*

HEBREWS 3:6 NIV

JULY 12

God may be invisible, but He's in touch. You may not be able to see Him, but He is in control. And that includes you—your circumstances. That includes what you've just lost. That includes what you've just gained. That includes all of life—past, present, future.

GROWING DEEP IN THE CHRISTIAN LIFE, P. 98

*Great is your love toward me; you have delivered me*
*from the depths of the grave.*

PSALM 86:13 NIV

JUNE 22

$O$thers won't care how much we know until they know how much we care.

COME BEFORE WINTER, P. 261

*Carry each other's burdens, and in this way*
*you will fulfill the law of Christ.*

GALATIANS 6:2 NIV

JULY 11

Although deity in flesh, not once did Jesus take unfair advantage of finite men and women who spent time with Him. Although himself omniscient, He gave others room to learn, to express themselves—even when they were dead wrong and He could have silenced them.

GROWING STRONG IN THE SEASONS OF LIFE, P. 384

*For even the Son of Man did not come to be served, but to serve, and to give his life as a ransom for many.*

MARK 10:45 NIV

JUNE 23

Return to this taproot of truth. Lean on it. Start today. It will hold you up and keep you strong. When it comes to a "final authority" in life, the Bible measures up.

GROWING DEEP IN THE CHRISTIAN LIFE, P. 66

*All men are like grass, and all their glory is like the flowers of the field; the grass withers and the flowers fall, but the word of the Lord stands forever.*

1 PETER 1:24,25 NIV

JULY 10

Doing is usually connected with a vocation or a career, how we make a living. Being is much deeper. It relates to character, who we are, and how we make a life.

GROWING STRONG IN THE SEASONS OF LIFE, P. 455

*Who may ascend the hill of the Lord? Who may stand in his holy place?*
*He who has clean hands and a pure heart, who does not lift up*
*his soul to an idol or swear by what is false.*

PSALM 24:3,4 NIV

JUNE 24

The sacrifice of the Lamb of God was once for all. We will never have to offer another sacrifice. It's not needed. His death on the cross finished the task.

GROWING DEEP IN THE CHRISTIAN LIFE, P. 256

*We have been made holy through the sacrifice of the body of Jesus Christ once for all.*

HEBREWS 10:10 NIV

# JULY 9

Don't just get older, get better. Live realistically. Give generously. Adapt willingly. Trust fearlessly. Rejoice daily.

STRIKE THE ORIGINAL MATCH, P. 182

*Gray hair is a crown of splendor; it is attained by a righteous life.*

PROVERBS 16:31 NIV

JUNE 25

**T**here can be no question about it,
marital intimacy is for sheer pleasure,
not just for enlarging the family.

STRIKE THE ORIGINAL MATCH, P. 77

*Let my lover come into his garden and
taste its choice fruits.*

SONG OF SONGS 4:16 NIV

JULY 8

You'll discover what life is about if you have correct insight into the nature of and conform your life to the character of the living God.

GROWING DEEP IN THE CHRISTIAN LIFE, P. 92

*The people that do know their God shall be strong, and do exploits.*

DANIEL 11:32 KJV

JUNE 26

Even the storms bear a message of encouragement for us: Deeper roots make for stronger lives.

GROWING STRONG IN THE SEASONS OF LIFE, P. 17

*And I pray that you, being rooted and established in love, may have power...to grasp how wide and long and high and deep is the love of Christ.*

EPHESIANS 3:17,18 NIV

JULY 7

# Becoming a contented person is a process, never an instant decision.

COME BEFORE WINTER, P. 301

*I know what it is to be in need, and I know what it is to have plenty. I have learned the secret of being content in any and every situation, whether well fed or hungry, whether living in plenty or in want.*

PHILIPPIANS 4:12 NIV

JUNE 27

Fight the tendency to prefer security to availability. In other words, quit hanging on to today's comfort. It will keep you from anticipating tomorrow's challenge.

GROWING WISE IN FAMILY LIFE, P. 267

*By faith Abraham...obeyed and went, even though he did not know where he was going.*

HEBREWS 11:8 NIV

JULY 6

The body of every believer that now resides in a casket, every believer torn apart by ravenous beasts, or by the elements of the sea, or by warfare, or awful murder will be received by Christ at His return.

GROWING DEEP IN THE CHRISTIAN LIFE, P. 271

*A time is coming when all who are in their graves will hear his voice and come out—those who have done good will rise to live, and those who have done evil will rise to be condemned.*

JOHN 5:28,29 NIV

JUNE 28

Busyness rapes relationships. It substitutes shallow frenzy for deep friendship. It promises satisfying dreams but delivers hollow nightmares. It feeds the ego but starves the inner man. It fills a calendar but fractures a family.

GROWING STRONG IN THE SEASONS OF LIFE, P. 554

*What does a man get for all the toil and anxious striving with which he labors under the sun?*

ECCLESIASTES 2:22,26 NIV

JULY 5

**W**e have become a generation of people who worship our work, who work at our play, and who play at our worship.

STRESS FRACTURES, P. 157

*Jesus went out to a mountainside to pray, and spent the night praying to God.*

LUKE 6:12 NIV

JUNE 29

God's hand is in your heartache. Yes, it is!
If you weren't important, do you think He would
take this long, and work this hard on your life?

ENCOURAGE ME, P. 36

*But now, O Lord, thou art our father; we are the clay,*
*and thou our potter; and we all are the work of thy hand.*

ISAIAH 64:8 KJV

# JULY 4

Thoughts form the thermostat which regulates what we accomplish in life. If I adjust my thermostat forward—to thoughts filled with vision, hope, and victory—I can count on that kind of day.

COME BEFORE WINTER, P. 238

*For thy mercy is great unto the heavens, and thy truth unto the clouds.*

PSALM 57:10 KJV

JUNE 30

God's glorious grace says: "Throw guilt and anxiety overboard—draw the anchor—trim the sails—man the rudder—a strong gale [of My Spirit] is coming!"

GROWING STRONG IN THE SEASONS OF LIFE, P. 374

*Repent, then, and turn to God, so that your sins may be wiped out, that times of refreshing may come from the Lord.*

ACTS 3:19 NIV

JULY 3